TRANSFORMING EVANGELISM

THE WESLEYAN WAY OF SHARING FAITH

HENRY H. KNIGHT III
F. DOUGLAS POWE, JR.

DISCIPLESHIP RESOURCES

PO BOX 340003 • NASHVILLE, TN 37203-0003
www.discipleshipresources.org

ISBN: 978-0-88177-485-6
Library of Congress Control Number 2005934554

We dedicate this book to our loved ones who have
stood by us in ministry:

ELOISE R. KNIGHT, SHERRI E. WOOD-POWE AND
FREDERICK DOUGLAS POWE, III

and to valued colleagues who have mentored us in evangelism:

GEORGE E. MORRIS AND W. STEPHEN GUNTER

ACKNOWLEGEMENTS

We want to thank Ms. Amy Hopmann for her assistance in
research and doing so much of the logistical work
to bring this book to publication.

A special thanks to Doug Powe's Postmodern Evangelism
class for their input into the manuscript.

TABLE OF CONTENTS

INTRODUCTION

Many people find the idea of practicing evangelism troubling. They are not eager to confront strangers with their personal faith, nor do they rejoice when people show up at their door to share their beliefs. They certainly cannot envision themselves speaking to thousands about Jesus in a football stadium. They may not be certain whether evangelism should be done at all, but if it is to be done they are very certain it is not to be done by them.

Part of the difficulty is how people understand what it means to evangelize. Many may envision it as confronting individuals with an argument for the gospel and an urgent call for decision. Whether they make an immediate decision for Christ determines whether they are "saved" or "lost." Either way, evangelism with them is done, and it is time to move on to the next person. We believe evangelism is more relational than confrontational, more communal than solitary, and is more a beginning point than an end. Evangelism involves not only sharing our faith with others, but also welcoming them into a community and enabling them to begin to grow in their faith. Above all evangelism is about love: God's love for us in Jesus, our love for our neighbor, and the invitation to receive and grow in a new life that is characterized by love.

In this book we want to present an evangelism of this kind. To do so we draw upon the expertise of one its greatest practitioners: John Wesley. Looking at what Wesley said and did in his day can give us insight and direction for our day. Wesley models an evangelism that reaches out and welcomes, invites and nurtures, and speaks to both head and heart.

9

By re-connecting to our Wesleyan tradition congregations can gain a new vision for evangelism, enabling them to be more faithful and effective in their ministry of sharing the good news. Above all by re-connecting with the Wesleyan tradition evangelism will be grounded in and motivated by the love of God.

A MESSAGE
WE LIVE

For by grace you have been saved through faith, and this is
not your own doing; it is the gift of God—not the result of
works, so that no one may boast. For we are what he has
made us, created in Christ Jesus for good works, which
God prepared beforehand to be our way of life. Ephesians
2:8-10

John Wesley preached around 40,000 sermons in his lifetime, bringing a message of good news to enormous crowds of listeners throughout Great Britain. Add to this the sermons preached by his brother Charles, his few clergy allies, and the small army of lay preachers he employed as his assistants, and it is clear the first Methodists produced an impressive amount of proclamation! And this does not include the witness of individual Methodists to their families, co-workers, and neighbors.

Just what message did all this highly organized evangelistic activity bring to the people of Great Britain? What motivated these Methodists—sometimes in the face of ridicule, persecution, or violence—to persist in their proclamation?

Wesley himself describes the motive for sharing the message:

We see—and who does not?—the numberless follies and miseries of our fellow creatures. We see on every side either men of no religion at all or men of a lifeless, formal religion. We are grieved at the sight, and should greatly rejoice if, by any means, we might convince some that there is a better religion to be attained, a religion worthy of God that gave it.[1]

The central motive was not recruiting new members for the church. It was not a reluctant yet dutiful obedience to a command of God. It was, instead, a profound gratitude to God and a deep compassion for others. It was the Methodists' experience of having received a message that had made all the difference in their own lives, and their resulting desire to share that message with others in the hope it would transform their lives as well.

What, then, was this "better religion" of which Wesley spoke?

And this we conceive to be no other than love: the love of God and all mankind; the loving God with all our heart and soul and strength, as having first loved *us,* as the fountain of all the good we have received and of all we ever hope to enjoy; and the loving every soul which God hath made . . . as our own soul.[2]

The Methodists, Wesley says, believe this love "to be the medicine of life, the never-failing remedy for all the evils of a disordered world. . . ."[3]

As we shall see, love is not the whole of the message, but it is at its heart. What was proclaimed was God's amazing love for us, and the promise that our lives can be so transformed that we can love God and others as we have been loved by God. "This," says Wesley, is the "religion we long to see established in the world: a religion of love and joy and peace, having its seat in the inmost soul, but ever showing itself by its fruits. . . ."[4]

What Salvation Is Not

We shall look at this message more closely in a moment. But it is already clear that when Wesley speaks of "true religion" or "salvation" there are two things he does not mean.

First, he does not understand religion to be a set of duties or activities that earn us a heavenly reward. It is surprising how many people today think Christianity is about being good so one can go to heaven when one dies. Many people already see themselves as good—that is, they have not committed any heinous crimes—and are therefore acceptable to God. Others put in a bit more effort, trying to be good citizens or active church members, believing that is the way to heaven.

Wesley instead sees salvation as a gift. As it says in Ephesians 2, salvation is "by grace," "a gift of God," and "not the result of works." It is received with gratitude, not earned with effort. Consequently the message of evangelism is not an exhortation to do better but to receive this gift through faith.

Second, Wesley does not understand salvation as a gift that leaves us unchanged. Here again, there are many who understand salvation as simply being forgiven of one's sins so that one goes to heaven when one dies. This becomes what Dietrich Bonhoeffer called "cheap grace," grace without discipleship. In Ron Sider's words, "Salvation becomes, not a life-transforming experience that reorients every corner of life, but a one-way ticket to heaven, and one can live like hell until one gets there."[5]

Wesley instead sees evangelism as a life-transforming gift. We are, as it says in Ephesians, "created in Christ Jesus for good works," intended by God "to be our way of life." Salvation is the gift of a new life, and such a gift cannot be stored away, it must be lived. Any evangelism which stops short of proclaiming that our lives are transformed is simply not the good news.

These two errors are in one sense opposites: one is salvation by works, the other is salvation apart from works and a changed life. But both of them share a fundamental misunderstanding of the message of salvation, one that is fatal to the gospel. Both believe salvation is about what happens when we die, that is, that we go to heaven rather than hell.

Wesley believes in going to heaven, but that is not for him the heart of salvation. Commenting on Ephesians 2:8 ("Ye are saved through faith") Wesley says the salvation spoken of in this text "is not a blessing which lies on the other side of death. . . . It is not something at a distance;" instead "it is a present thing, a blessing which, through the free mercy of God, ye are now in possession of."[6] It is the gift of a new life, a life we have in the present, and which death cannot take from us. It is heaven in the heart.

The Message of Salvation

The central message of Wesley and his Methodists can be summarized in five affirmations.

SALVATION IS OFFERED TO EVERYONE

Unlike some in the awakening in the eighteenth century, Wesley insisted this new life is offered to every person in the world. He believed God's grace is at work in every human heart, enabling and inviting persons to turn toward God. This means God has already been preparing people for the good news of salvation even before they actually hear it.

What underlies this is a profound sense of God's universal love. It would be impossible to overstate the significance of God's love for Wesley's theology and ministry, as well as for Charles Wesley's hymns. The ultimate expression of God's love was the cross of Jesus Christ. Charles Wesley puts it this way:

> O Love divine, what hast thou done!
> The immortal God hath died for me!
> The Father's co-eternal Son bore all my sins
>   upon the tree.
> Th' immortal God for me hath died:
> My Lord, my love, is crucified.[7]

What this means is that each person—every one of us—is of infinite worth to God. There was no cost too high, no effort too great, for God to reach out to us in love. In a world in which millions of people are being told they are worth little or nothing, this is good news indeed!

EVERYONE NEEDS SALVATION

Not only does God love every person and offer them new life, but everyone needs the life that only God can give. What underlies this is a corresponding sense of the universality of human sin. Wesley believes we have a problem we cannot fix, a disease we cannot cure.

It is not just that we are guilty, though we are. We are indeed responsible for all those thoughts and actions that are contrary to God's love. But sin is not only what we do, it is a condition: we *are* sinners. As such, we need not only forgiveness but transformation.

How is this good news? Just as in dealing with sickness or addiction, to know the truth is the first step to renewed health. God's judgment is not meant to be an ending but the possibility of a new beginning. It is diagnosis more than condemnation; or perhaps better stated, it is condemnation only for those who reject the diagnosis.

We Can Be Forgiven

God deals with the guilt of sin by offering forgiveness, or justification. We receive this gift through faith alone, trusting in what God has done for us in the cross of Jesus Christ. As a result we are reconciled to God—we enter into a relationship with God based not on fear of punishment but in gratitude for God's incomprehensible love.

We live, then, as people who have been forgiven. We move from a life of regret and dutiful obedience to one of peace, joy and profound gratitude.

We Can Receive New Life

God deals with the condition of sin by offering a new life of love, or sanctification. We receive this gift through faith alone as well. As a result we grow in the knowledge and love of God, being increasingly conformed to the image of God.

We live, then, as people who love God and others as we have been loved by God. This new life affects everything about us—our relationships, values, lifestyle, and commitments. We desire to see the world as God sees it, and to act in ways that bring God's love and justice to bear on the situations around us.

We Can Be Truly Happy

We have a happiness that cannot be found through the pursuit of wealth or fame, or the attainment of status or power. It does not come through immersion in those "pleasures" traditionally deemed sinful. It is not even the happiness that comes from friends and family, though it is compatible with it.

This happiness is peace and joy in the Holy Spirit. It comes from being in a relationship with the God who loves us so much. It also comes from being increasingly transformed into the persons we were created to be, in accordance with the intent of our Creator.

We live, then, as a people who have a depth of happiness that is only possible through Jesus Christ. Since this happiness comes from God, nothing can take it from us, because nothing, not even death, can put an end to God's love or take away the life God gives. As Paul says,

> I am convinced that neither death, nor life, nor angels, nor rulers, nor things present, nor things to come, nor powers, nor height, nor depth, nor anything else in all creation, will be able to separate us from the love of God in Christ Jesus our Lord. (Rom 8:38-39)

A Definition

We can now offer a definition of evangelism in the Wesleyan tradition:

> *Evangelism is our sharing and inviting others to experience the good news that God loves us and invites us into a transforming relationship through which we are forgiven, receive new life, and are restored to the image of God, which is love.*

Wesleyan evangelism is firmly grounded on what God has done for our salvation in the life, death, and resurrection of Jesus Christ, and relies completely on the presence and power of the Holy Spirit. The good news is shared through proclamation and testimony, and experienced in community through vital worship, caring fellowship, regular personal devotions, and acts of compassion and justice to others.

Wesleyan evangelism, then, has new life as its goal, but utilizes

17

a variety of means to enable persons to both hear and experience this new life. In the chapters to come we will say more about this rich set of evangelistic practices. Our hope is that this book will aid Christians and churches in faithfully and effectively sharing this promise of new life with others.

Questions

1. Should we be concerned to share the good news of Jesus Christ with others, and if so, why?

2. Why do so many people think of Christianity as a set of obligations to obtain a reward in the life to come rather than the gift of a new life in the present?

3. In the brief sketch of Wesley's message of salvation in this chapter, what surprised you? What did or did not make sense? Do you find it a challenge and/or a source of hope?

4. If someone asked you just what the good news of Jesus Christ is, what would you tell them? If they asked what salvation is, how would you respond?

5. If someone asked you what difference faith in Jesus Christ has made in your life, what would you say?

A JOURNEY
WE BEGIN

I am the true vine, and my Father is the vinegrower. He
removes every branch in me that bears no fruit. Every
branch that bears fruit he prunes to make it bear more
fruit. You have already been cleansed by the word that I
have spoken to you. Abide in me as
I abide in you. Just as the branch cannot bear fruit
by itself unless it abides in the vine, neither can
you unless you abide in me. I am the vine, you are the
branches. Those who abide in me and I in them bear
much fruit, because apart from me you can
do nothing. John 15:1-5

The new life is about bearing fruit: faith, hope, humility, and
especially love. In order to do that, it must be rooted in and
nourished by a relationship with Jesus Christ. To receive
and grow in this new life, we must abide in Christ.

The early Methodists understood their need to abide in Christ.
They sought to keep to a set of spiritual disciplines designed to keep
them open to God's grace, and they met once a week in small
groups called classes to discuss that discipline and be held accountable to it.

To change the metaphor, they understood the Christian life to be a journey whose goal is for love of God and neighbor to fill their hearts and govern their lives. The discipline and class meetings kept them on the road toward that goal. When the Christian life is understood this way, evangelism cannot mark the end of the journey. Instead, it has to be a means to help people begin the journey.

All too often evangelism is not seen this way. Often evangelism is understood as imparting information—a plan of salvation, for example—that leads to a decision. The person who makes a positive decision is then called "saved." If the decision is viewed as the goal, or if all this remains only on the intellectual level, then this form of evangelism falls far short of the new life promised by God. But if the decision leads to a process of formation and growth, it can be the beginning of a life that abides in Christ.

Sometimes evangelism is seen not as leading to a decision but to evoking an experience. The person who has this experience of conversion is said to be "saved." But again, if having the experience is viewed as the goal, then this too falls short of the new life promised by God. Feelings, as we know, come and go. But if a conversion experience leads to a genuine change of heart, which continues to be nurtured by grace, then it will be the beginning of a new life that bears much fruit.

To speak of the Christian life as a journey does not set aside instantaneous conversion. Wesley himself rarely used the word "conversion," preferring instead to speak of justification and the new birth, or more comprehensively, of salvation. He describes salvation as *both* instantaneous and gradual, with justification and new birth as a transformation by God that flows from and leads to growth over time.

Wesley's insistence that forgiveness is received and a new life begins in an event of transformation underscores that all of this is by grace alone. Speaking of the faith in Jesus Christ through which we receive this gift of forgiveness and new life, Wesley says

> No man is able to work it, in himself. It is a work of omnipotence. It requires no less power thus to quicken a dead soul than to raise a body that lies in the grave. It is a new creation, and none can create a soul anew but he who at first created the heavens and the earth.[1]

If this is true—that conversion is a work of God that is received—it has huge implications for how we practice evangelism. Eddie Fox and George Morris, in their book *Faith-Sharing*, insist "that it is God who converts." The goal of evangelism is not to convert anyone, but to share the good news we have received with others. "Evangelizing," they say, "is not something we do *to* people but something we do *with* the gospel."[2]

So conversion is a work of God through the power of the Holy Spirit. It is, however, both preceded and followed by a process of formation, also through the Spirit. When people responded to early Methodist preaching or personal testimonies, they were enrolled in a small group where they began to practice spiritual disciplines. That is, they were placed in an environment designed to help them be open and receptive to God's work in their lives.

What they were seeking was the new life which God had promised. Initially they sought to obey God out of fear of God's judgment and an obligation to do good, what Wesley calls the "faith of a servant." Through this they came to see more clearly their need to rely on God. After some time—for many, over two years—they experienced for themselves God's forgiveness and received the new life of love. Now they began to obey God not out of fear and duty but love and gratitude, growing daily in love in response to the love they have received. Now, with the "faith of a child of God," they began to seek the promise of Christian perfection, when God's love would fully fill their hearts and govern their lives.

Beginning the Journey

Let us look more closely at how those who responded to early Methodist evangelism were set upon the journey of the Christian life—how they began to "abide in Christ." The spiritual disciplines they began to practice were what Wesley called the "Rules of the United Societies." They consisted of three general rules.

The first was to do no harm "by avoiding evil in every kind; especially that which is most generally practiced." That is, Methodists were to turn from ways of life that, however considered normal by the larger culture, are contrary to God's will.

The second was to do good "by being in every kind merciful after their power; as they have opportunity, doing good of every possible sort . . . to both the bodies and souls of others." This included feeding the hungry, clothing the naked, visiting or helping those who are sick or in prison, and instructing and encouraging persons in the gospel. These were "works of mercy" through which was expressed compassion to the neighbor.

The third was to attend the ordinances of God such as "the public worship of God; the ministry of the word, either read or expounded, the Supper of the Lord; private prayer; searching the Scriptures; and fasting, or abstinence."[3] These were "works of piety" through which love for God was expressed.

Anyone who has tried to begin a daily devotional life, much less make major lifestyle changes, would testify how difficult something like this is. This is why early Methodists did not try to do it alone. Instead, they came together in weekly class meetings to report on how well they had done in keeping to the discipline the preceding week, and to receive advice and encouragement for the week ahead. The weekly meeting was a powerful incentive to enable the Methodists to keep to their discipline.

This was important, for, just as we do today, they faced many obstacles in life that would draw them away from their journey. Wesley saw us as "encompassed on all sides with persons and things that tend to draw us from our centre,"[4] which is God. This process of being drawn away Wesley calls "dissipation"; it results in our being "habitually inattentive to the presence and will" of God.[5] We become "practical atheists"[6] who say we believe in God but actually live as if there were no God.

It is important to recognize that the things which draw us away from God are not only temptations to sin. Busy schedules, never-ending deadlines, and worries and concerns can also draw us from God. Even things we rightly count as good—church, family, work—can move to the center of our lives and push God to the side.

Here we can see why the discipline was so effective: it kept people focused on God and on their neighbor, counteracting dissipation. This is why any practice of evangelism that stops short of placing persons in a discipline is sub-Wesleyan, and runs the danger of letting the pressures of life undermine a new commitment to God.

According to George G. Hunter III, the Wesleyan model of formation is an effective way to communicate the gospel to modern, secular people. He describes six stages experienced by persons who adopt Christianity:

> First, people become *aware*, or newly aware, of Christianity—not as an abstraction but as a particular movement, group of people, church, or truth claim. Second, people perceive the *relevance* of that . . . form of Christianity. . . . They respond, third, with *active interest*, in which they (perhaps) ask questions, read a book, attend a seminar, or visit a church's worship service. Fourth, they enter upon a *trial* state, . . . trying it on for size. Fifth, they consciously *adopt the faith*, and are publicly baptized and/or received into church membership. . . .[7]

This is followed by a sixth stage, *reinforcement*, which occurs through the discipling ministries of the church.

The similarities of the process of conversion to that of the early Methodists are striking, and are explicitly noted by Hunter.[8] We would describe the similarities this way. People became aware of the Methodists and were awakened by their message. When they responded with interest, they were enrolled in a class meeting. Through practicing the spiritual disciplines, they entered into a relationship with God which eventually led to their experiencing forgiveness and new birth, as much being adopted by God as their adopting the faith. Reinforcement occurred as they continued in their relationship with God through the spiritual disciplines.

But apart from the similarities, the larger point is that the Wesleyan pattern of formation is as relevant today as it was in the eighteenth century. This underscores the importance for Wesleyan evangelism to be linked to small groups, spiritual disciplines, and Christian formation.

There is a notable attempt to recover the Wesleyan spiritual disciplines and class meetings for today in Covenant Discipleship.[9] One difference is that, instead of Wesley's three rules, this contemporary version allows each group to develop their own covenant around four general areas: acts of compassion, justice, devotion, and worship. To be a member of a Covenant Discipleship group with regular meetings to discuss the covenant to which all members are accountable would have the same sort of benefit as Wesley's class meeting.

There also have been several attempts to rethink evangelism in order to link it more clearly with entering into Christian formation. The most common definitions of evangelism do not do this—they are centered on proclaiming the good news of Jesus Christ or in sharing our faith with another. William Abraham argues such definitions are too narrow in that they stop short of what is necessary for a person to be a Christian. He defines evangelism instead "as that set of intentional activities which is governed by the goal of initiating people into the Kingdom of God for the first time."[10] Those activities are six in number: conversion, baptism, the rule of life (beginning to learn to love God and neighbor), the rule of faith (basic Christian teaching structured around a historic creed), life in the Spirit (empowerment with spiritual gifts to work in service to God's kingdom), and spiritual disciplines (such as prayer, fasting, and the Lord's Supper).

Scott Jones both builds upon and revises Abraham. He defines evangelism "as that set of loving, intentional activities governed by the goal of initiating persons into Christian discipleship in response to the reign of God."[11] To Abraham's six activities he adds a seventh: learning to share our faith with others.

The strength of these understandings of evangelism is they lead us to ask what sorts of practices of initiation are necessary for a person to become a Christian. They are Wesleyan in that they link proclamation and faith-sharing with Christian formation. That is, they insure we are placed in a transforming relationship and begin the practices that enable us to live out our new life in Christ. A response to the message of good news places one on a lifelong journey of faith, and enables one to abide in Christ.

Evangelism and Baptism

Should persons who are baptized be evangelized? If baptism is a rite of entry into the family of God, then doesn't baptism make one a Christian? And if that is the case, shouldn't evangelism be directed toward those who are not baptized?

Wesley was preaching the good news to a largely baptized audience. He was accused of trying to convert people who were already Christian. Yet he clearly did not see it that way.

While Wesley strongly affirmed baptism as a sacrament through which God works, and did not doubt that persons baptized as infants were born anew and made members of the family of God, he doubted very much that many as adults were Christian in any real sense. The reason was they did not manifest the new life that is the mark of a Christian, most especially love for God and neighbor

To the sinner who says "I defy your . . . doctrine; I need not be born again. I was born again when I was baptized. What! Would you have me deny my baptism?" Wesley responds "you have already denied your baptism, and that in a most effectual manner. You have denied it a thousand . . . times; and you do still day by day," by living a way of life that is contrary to God's will and not governed by love for God and neighbor.[12]

The sad truth is that, like the prodigal son, we can leave home, move to a far country, and adopt a way of life contrary to that of a Christian. That does not make us unbaptized—it does not nullify God's promises and claim upon our life. But it does mean our hearts and lives no longer reflect the love of God. We need to hear the good news that we can be forgiven and enter into the new life God gives to us, and thus fulfill the promise of God given in our baptism.

The problem Wesley faced of so many persons baptized yet not Christian in heart and life might be lessened by placing baptism itself within a process of formation. That is what the church did in the early centuries of Christianity. Seekers were enrolled in the catechumenate, where they regularly prayed, served, worshipped, and heard the word preached ("catechumen" means "hearer"). When they were ready to become Christians, often after two or three years, they underwent an intense time of prayer and fasting that led to baptism.

The similarities with Wesley's practice have not gone unnoticed, including by Wesley himself. He saw the discipline and classes as a revival of the catechemenate, although unlike the catechumens in the early church, most of those in classes had already been baptized and participation in a class was lifelong.

Some have sought to revive this early church practice of Christian initiation for our day. Daniel Benedict describes it as a process with three steps for adult seekers: evangelism, formation and instruction, and baptism as the sacrament of initiation. For infants the formation and instruction would follow baptism, and lead to a later profession of faith. In both cases, the link between baptism and new life is secured through Christian formation.[13]

Robert E. Webber defines evangelism not just as the entry but as encompassing the entire process, from becoming a seeker to baptism and incorporation into the full life of the church. He adds an element at the end in which the newly baptized discover their spiritual gifts and become engaged in ministry.[14] These contemporary attempts to recover the early church practice of Christian initiation can contribute to Wesleyan evangelism provided they don't just stop at baptism but lead into a lifelong process of Christian formation.

Whatever its exact definition, evangelism in the Wesleyan tradition can never be divorced from formation. For seekers, Christian formation both precedes conversion (and baptism) and then follows from it. Wesleyan evangelism enables us to begin a journey of faith, hope, and love. It has as its goal our entry into a new life in which we abide in Christ, and therefore have lives that bear much fruit.

Questions

1. What has been your understanding of evangelism? How does it compare to Wesley's?

2. What in our world today might lead to dissipation and result in our no longer abiding in Christ? What can we do to lessen the danger of dissipation?

3. If someone responded to evangelism and came to your church, what opportunities for Christian formation would they find? Are there ways you can think of to improve this area?

4. How do you think evangelism and baptism are related? Would recovering something like the catechumenate of the early church strengthen the impact of baptism in the life of a Christian?

A COMMUNITY WE ENTER

Awe came upon everyone, because many wonders and signs were being done by the apostles. All who believed were together and had all things in common; they would sell their possessions and goods and distribute the proceeds to all, as any had need. Day by day, as they spent much time together in the temple, they broke bread at home and ate their food with glad and generous hearts, praising God and having the goodwill of all the people. And day by day the Lord added to their number those who were being saved. Acts 2:43-47

Wesley not only emphasized the need for personal transformation when we become Christians, he also emphasized the important role the community plays in that transformation. A community is called to live out in practical ways the love, mercy and justice of God. For Wesley, this means a community should be both inviting and sustain believers on the journey. The challenge many Christian church communities face today is the balance between being inviting to others and sustaining current members on their journey.

Two quick stories illustrate the challenge many churches face today. A preacher was moved to a new congregation and decided to visit incognito to learn about the congregation. The preacher decided to dress in old torn jeans and holy sneakers. He entered the church and noticed people staring at him strangely. A man came up to him and said the church with the free Sunday meals is down the street. No one wanted to sit next to him on the pew and he was not even offered a bulletin. Needless to say the preacher was very disappointed by the congregation's reaction. In a few weeks when the preacher came dressed in nice slacks and nice shoes the congregation was very receptive. They were shocked to hear the preacher was the person who visited a few weeks earlier and was treated so poorly. This church community needs to rediscover what it meant to be inviting.

A family faithfully attended church all of their lives and from outside appearances they seemed like the perfect "All-American" family. A tragedy occurred when the daughter died suddenly. The congregation was shocked and offered condolences, but never really went beyond surface comments. Many in the congregation did not know the family because they only saw them on Sunday, and others thought because they attended church regularly their faith would get them through. When the family stopped attending church after a month one or two people called, but even they stopped after a couple of weeks. It did not take long for this family to be forgotten almost entirely by most in the congregation. This church community needs to rediscover what it means to sustain believers on their journey. A Wesleyan paradigm for communal evangelism offers hope to both of these churches.

Social Holiness

Wesley once claimed, "There is no holiness but social holiness."[1] The phrase social holiness for some today at first glance may seem like Wesley is advocating for a political agenda. He is not advocating for a political agenda as we think about it today, but Wesley is arguing that transformation is about more than just one's personal life. Wesley believes communities and even society can be transformed into the image of Christ and all things created new. Thus, the role of the Christian community is to help individuals become more Christlike.

For Wesley, a Christian community should be inviting to others so that individuals can begin the journey to develop a relationship with Jesus as well as sustain them on that journey. Christian communities must actively reach out to those not in the community helping them to enter into it. The act of reaching out to others is an invitation to begin a process of being made whole by Jesus the Christ. To be made whole is to become so filled with the love of Christ that our relationships with others are radically transformed for the better. In a sense, social holiness represents a community so radically transformed by the love of Christ for the better that they are inviting to others by their "words, deeds and signs."[2]

At the same time, it is the community that must sustain believers in their Christian journey. The Christian community has the responsibility of keeping the relationship with Jesus alive so that believers will continue to grow in grace. One of the dangers any Christian community faces is becoming like the church at Laodicea, "neither cold nor hot." (Rev 3:16). The challenge the Christian community faces is how to keep the fire burning so that the love of Christ continues to be lived out in a transformational manner. An evangelistic community within the Wesleyan tradition always is seeking to be more Christlike, which means finding ways to strengthen their relationship with God and neighbor. For

Wesley, social holiness is an on-going process that helps the community to deepen its relationship with God and neighbor.

There is indeed no holiness without social holiness. Although we accept Jesus into our personal lives, we live out what it means to be in a relationship with Jesus in community with others. The community has the dual responsibility of inviting others to a personal relationship with Jesus and helping them to sustain this relationship as they are re-formed into the image of Christ. How can a community be both inviting and sustain believers—becoming an evangelistic community?

A Wesleyan Paradigm for Community

In Acts 2:43-47 we have a glimpse of a particular Christian community. While by no means the only Christian community in the New Testament, it does offer us a window through which we can think paradigmatically about the notion of an evangelistic Wesleyan community. We will highlight five points from the text that gives shape to such a paradigm.

BELIEVERS WERE TOGETHER (ACTS 2:44)

The text states that the believers were together and this is important because it is the only way we can move beyond having shallow relationships with one another. Wesley's evangelistic approach centers on relationality. He expected the People called Methodists to gather together often to encourage, strengthen and challenge each other to continue being faithful. In chapter two we talked about the importance of the class meetings for helping people begin their journey. One of the reasons Wesley started the meetings was he felt the "bulk of parishioners a mere rope of sand with no Christian connection between them."[3] The classes were instrumental in building a connection between the believers.

A question for us today is, "Are we (the bulk of parishioners) a mere rope of sand with no Christian connection?" We gather on Sunday or some other day of the week for worship and engage in polite conversation with each other. An evangelistic community, however, needs to do more than gather for worship one day a week. It should be a community of believers committed to growing in the love of Christ together. It is a community that has developed relationships with each other that move beyond "politically correct dialogue." Wesley attempted to build a community of believers that lived up to the hope of strengthening, challenging and encouraging each other on the Christian journey. They understood to become this type of a community they had to be together.

DISTRIBUTED PROCEEDS TO THE NEEDY (ACTS 2:45)

The text suggests that the believers did not come together just for themselves, but were concerned for others. An evangelistic community should sustain believers on the journey by coming together, but this community must also reach out to others. The People called Methodists collected a penny a week to give to those in need.[4] In fact, class members were encouraged to ask their neighbor for a penny to help with those members unable to give.[5] By reaching out to those not in the classes Wesley created an inviting community, which made evangelistic practices a part of its nature and not an additional responsibility.

Wesley challenges us today to create an inviting community. Size has nothing to do with reaching out to others. Many of the classes were not large and many of the participants were poor. Yet, the People called Methodists still sought to reach out to others in love. An evangelistic community avoids the snare of focusing on its own needs and remembers it has a responsibility to demonstrate the love of Christ to others. A Christian community that ceases to reach out to others is one that will eventually cease.

BREAKING OF BREAD (ACTS 2:46)

The text discusses the fact that the believers broke bread at home and ate with glad and generous hearts. This part of the text is connected to point one above where we talked about believers being together. The difference in this part of the text is that the believers are breaking bread with each other at home. The point is the believers are deepening their relationships with each other. Although it is not a direct correlation, the idea behind the love feast served a similar purpose for Wesley. Wesley felt by participating in love feasts he was continuing an early form of the Christian "love meal."[6] It was a way for the participants to deepen their relationships with God and each other by the sharing of the feasts.

The question for us today is, "Are we really willing to break bread with one another?" The act of breaking bread together signals a different type of relationship than some of us want in the church. An evangelistic community has to find ways to bring down the walls separating believers so they can "break bread together." When the walls come down and a community can eat with glad tidings it will attract others who will want to become a part of the community. Although the breaking of bread may seem like an insignificant act, the ramifications are significant for a community seeking to deepen their relationship with God, each other and others.

Praising God (Acts 2:47)

The text says the believers were praising God. Why is it important that the text point out the believers were praising God? First, Wesley reminds us that we have not accomplished anything by our own actions—it is only by the grace of God a community flourishes. God deserves our praise. Second, Wesley realized the important role praise played in attracting those outside of the faith. Wesley investigated a praise service at Kingswood that he eventually endorsed making Kingswood the model for similar gatherings in other cities extending the opportunity for the word of God to find the heart of non-believers.[7] Thus, praising God both reminds the community about the importance of the grace of God and opens up the community to those in need of God's grace. A community of praise plays a central role as a conduit to helping those outside the faith to discover God's love and those inside the faith to be assured of God's love.

A lot of churches emphasize praise services today. Yet, Wesley reminds us *why* we praise God. An evangelistic community is one that understands its dependence on the grace of Jesus the Christ and not its own works. The fact that a church may have talented musicians and singers to create a praise service does not mean a particular church is praising God better than another. If God is not recognized as the giver of the gifts, then the praise service has missed its mark. We must be careful not to get caught-up in our abilities and remember to respond to the Holy Spirit which guides us. Those inside and outside of the community should genuinely experience God's grace and not something contrived by human effort.

Adding to the Number (Acts 2:47)

The text says "day by day the Lord added to their number." Because the early church community was inviting and sought to meet the needs of others, God added to their numbers. One of the strengths of the Wesleyan revival was it reached out to those the state church tended to ignore. Wesley preached in the fields fighting his own initial reservations about such a practice and was able to reach many individuals who did not attend church regularly. Wesley eventually believed it was more important for the gospel to reach those in need than for the gospel to be preached within a particular structure. Wesley, however, did not just preach and leave the people on their own; he developed a relationship with them by inviting them to class meetings. An evangelistic community is one that is relational and invites others to hear and experience the gospel.

Are we invitational in our churches today? Do we help new believers to grow in the faith? The truth is some churches are stuck in a maintenance mode and stopped inviting others to experience the love of Christ. Other churches are inviting, but are so focused on growth they have forgotten the need to help believers to grow in the faith. An evangelistic church must be both inviting and help new believers to grow in the faith. We inherit from Wesley a relational model that encourages us to be both inviting and to help believers to grow in the faith.

In general an evangelistic community within the Wesleyan tradition has a lot in common with the early church community presented in Acts. Wesley incorporated the early church theme of inviting outsiders while sustaining the believers in the faith into his evangelistic ministry. Wesley gives us hints on how to form our church communities today to become more evangelistic. The bottom line, for Wesley, is the church community is about relationships—helping outsiders and insiders to better love God and neighbor.

An Inviting Community

In Chapter Two we introduced the classes and the importance of the classes to the Methodist movement. The classes helped Wesley to build a structure where one could maintain the essence of a personal relationship with Jesus, but the evidence of this relationship was public and social.[8] Class members were expected to do works of piety and works of mercy. Works of piety are one way of strengthening the personal relationship with Jesus through reading scripture, prayer, etc. Works of mercy are a way of engaging in public witness by showing compassion and acting justly toward our neighbors. An inviting community is one that shows compassion and acts justly toward its neighbor, yet always remembering the message of salvation so central to the gospel.

In Chapter One, we touched on Wesley's understanding of salvation as a present blessing, something that can be enjoyed in this life. Wesley certainly maintains salvation is also about seeking an eternal home in heaven, but to limit salvation only to an other-worldly hope is to miss the blessing of God's grace in this life. If the focus of salvation is not strictly other-worldly, then it follows, for Wesley, what we do in terms of addressing the needs of the entire person is critical. An inviting community does not evangelize to the soul while ignoring the physical needs of people. Moreover, an inviting community does not address social issues while ignoring their responsibility to present the gospel to people. Because Wesley argues salvation is a present blessing he destroys simplistic either/or options that many congregations fall into today.

For example, a congregation that decides to do outreach to single parents trying to make ends meet each month by simply addressing their spiritual needs has not considered the entire person. The congregation may overlook their possible need for daycare, meals and transportation to name just a few concerns. A congregation taking the opposite approach and designing outreach programs that solely focus on social issues, and not presenting the gospel is also a distortion. The concern for the spiritual needs of a person is critical, but Wesley understood the importance of ministering to the entire person. If the hope is to help individuals to become transformed into the image of God, then an evangelistic community has to avoid the snare of either/or options and focus on the entire person.

At the beginning of this chapter we talked about social holiness and the renewal of the image of God meaning being filled with the love of Christ. For Wesley, being renewed in the image of God can become a testimony to society.[9] The testimony in this instance is lived out in the manner a community reflects Jesus' love for others.[10] An evangelistic community cannot be inviting if it is not a living testimony to Jesus' love for us. It is one thing to proclaim Jesus' love, but it is another to live it.

For Wesley, an inviting community engages in concrete expressions of its faith by reaching out to others. Wesley in his own ministry reached out to the poor, undereducated and those in prisons. Reaching out to the marginalized, for Wesley, did not mean sending money and thinking one had done all one should. Wesley insisted upon actual physical contact with those who were in need.[11] In discussing visiting the sick, Wesley said:

> By the sick, I do not mean only those that keep in their bed, or that are sick in the strictest sense. Rather I would include all such as are in a state of affliction, whether of mind or body; and that, whether they are good or bad, whether they fear God or not. 'But is there need of visiting them in person? May we not relieve the at a distance?'. . . . The word which we render *visit*, in its literal

acceptation, means, to 'look upon.' And this, you well know, cannot be done, unless you are present with them.[12]

The lesson for an inviting community is to make contact with those we reach out to in an effort to make them a part of the community. Certainly, some situations will warrant that physical contact is not always possible. But an inviting community within the Wesleyan tradition cannot settle for detached contact with those outside of the community because being in relationship with another means being present with them.

For Wesley, an inviting community seeks to transform itself and others through love. The mirroring of God's love, mercy, and justice to others is what every Christian community should practice. Our claim to love God must translate into some form of a concrete practice with another that becomes a public testimony. Wesley was successful in reaching others and inviting them into the community because he brought them the hope of God's love and forgiveness. This did not excuse one from changing; in fact it should compel one to want to change because of God's love. An evangelistic community is one that understands the power of God's love to transform others and itself and to be renewed into the image of God.

We began this section by talking about the classes and the important role they played in establishing a public witness. The classes were instrumental in shaping the type of Christian community that Wesley felt could make a difference in non-believers' lives. For non-believers it was a place where they could go to learn more about the love of Christ and God's forgiveness. But the classes not only invited others into the community, they sustained the members on their journey.

A Sustaining Community

For believers, community was a place to be held accountable to live out the gospel in deeds and not strictly words. Wesley remarked:

> But as much as we endeavored to watch over each other, we soon found some who did not 'live the gospel.' I do not know that any hypocrites were crept in; for indeed there was no temptation: But several grew cold, and gave way to sins which had long easily beset them.[13]

The classes were a place where the People called Methodists could learn to live out their faith by being accountable to one another. The hope was individuals would be sustained in the faith by requiring them to give an account of how they were doing each week. We probably think Wesley's idea of giving an account to someone about how we lived during week is strange. Yet, we can learn from Wesley the importance of sharing our burdens with each other and praying for each other.

To help foster community Wesley encouraged the participants to speak truthfully about the state of their souls.[14] Building community means taking a risk at some level that you trust the others in the community. If we want others to stay in community with us we must learn to hear their concerns and to share our burdens with them. A church cannot build this type of a community if it only comes together for worship on Sunday. One of the strengths of Wesley's class meetings was it helped believers to stay strong in the faith because they knew others were walking with them on the journey. If we are going to sustain believers in the faith today, then we need to find ways to reclaim partnerships with others. Bringing someone into the community and leaving them to struggle on their own is not what it means to be an evangelistic community.

What is it that an evangelistic community hopes will occur with those who enter the community? For Wesley, it was that their affections and tempers would be transformed by God so that they could become new creatures in Christ. We would not use the terms affections and tempers today, instead we would use terms like character and dispositions. The transformation of one's disposition and character does not happen overnight; it takes place over time. The truth for most of us is that God will be transforming our dispositions and character all our lives as we seek to be renewed into the image of God.

It is only by God transforming our disposition and character that it is possible to redefine our relationships with God and neighbor. Wesley often used the metaphor of a disease to describe how our dispositions are not properly aligned with God. It is only through being renewed into the image of God that we can begin to find healing and experience true transformation. A sustaining community is one place where individuals should find others willing to help them remain open to God's healing transformation in their lives. The community is responsible for helping individuals to stay faithful to being renewed into the image of God.

For example, no matter what size a church is it can establish prayer groups or prayer partners as a means of helping individuals to stay connected. The idea is the same as Wesley's class structure where people were able to sustain one another through prayer. It also is a way to make sure new members can get connected into the church. The purpose is not to force anyone to share unwillingly, but to establish relationships with others that will be meaningful for the Christian journey. One of the challenges today is we live in a society where many people want to stay anonymous, and this is true even when it comes to church. Yet, Wesley pushes against this notion of anonymity calling us to develop a deeper sense of community than many of us feel comfortable doing.

The bottom line is a sustaining community helps new and old believers to experience some form of inward change. The process of this transformation is important because it helps the community to develop a pattern of practices that enables it to be more inviting. The inward change should manifest itself into some form of outward action, such as justice, mercy, and truth. A community that continues to experience an inward transformation that manifests itself into outward action is able to mirror God's love, mercy, and justice to others in the world. It is a community that testifies to what Wesley means by social holiness.

Wesley makes the connection plain when he writes:

> By salvation I mean, not barely, according to the vulgar notion, deliverance from hell, or going to heaven: but a present deliverance from sin, a restoration of the soul to its primitive health, its original purity; a recovery of the divine nature; the renewal of our souls after the image of God, in righteousness and true holiness, in justice, mercy and truth. This implies all holy and heavenly tempers, and by consequence all holiness of conversation.[15]

In contrast to our day, Wesley's use of the term "conversation" not only means talking, but means "all types of human conduct."[16] The point is a sustaining community develops a pattern of practices by being renewed into the image of God that enables it to mirror these practices publicly. An evangelistic community within the Wesleyan tradition understands the importance of inward transformation as a process to becoming an inviting community. Wesley wanted the People Called Methodists to understand salvation as a lifelong journey involving both inward and outward change. He was successful as an evangelist because he formed communities where people developed a pattern of practices making inward and outward transformation possible.

Love Feast

We talked about the importance of breaking bread together in the early church and how Wesley's use of the love feast was somewhat similar. The love feast was designed to allow individuals to give their personal testimonies and for them to share bread with one another modeled after the ancient church. The bread was symbolic because it was understood to provide nourishment for the community as a whole as they journeyed together. Following is a hymn used by the classes for love feast that illuminates the point of nourishment and journeying together:

Let us join ('tis God commands),
Let us join our hearts and hands;
Help to gain our calling's hope,
Build we each the other up.
God his blessing shall dispense,
God shall crown his ordinance,
Meet in his appointed ways,
Nourish us with social grace.

Let us then brethren love,
Faithfully his gifts improve,
Carry on the earnest strife,
Walk in holiness of life.

Still forget the things behind,
Follow Christ in heart and mind,
Toward the mark unwearied press,
Seize the crown of righteousness![17]

The love feast was a way for the community to come together and celebrate the journey it was taking to "walk in holiness of life."[18] It was a way for the community to encourage each other in a different way by sharing testimonies with each other. A service for a love feast is still in the United Methodist Book of Worship, but most churches today do not offer this service. Some churches could benefit by reclaiming this service as an integral part of the life of the church. The service represents what it means to struggle together as a community and that God's grace is active in that struggle. It represents the delicate balance an evangelistic community seeks to maintain between invitation (through testimonies) and sustaining (continued nourishment) each other in the faith. It is an opportunity to break bread together and to feast so that all may "taste and see that the LORD is good."

Community Today

The theme of this chapter has been maintaining the balance between inviting others into community and sustaining them in community. We highlighted how one early church community in Acts was able to do so. Moreover, we discussed the similarities between the early Acts church community and some of Wesley's practices. As we think in terms of evangelism for church communities today it is important that they seek to maintain the balance between inviting others and sustaining them in the faith.

One community today that maintains the balance we are arguing for in this chapter is firefighters. Firefighters are not a church community, but churches can learn from how firefighters form and maintain community. Firefighters, because they must live together, break bread together and learn to trust each other for the purpose of fighting fires—they create a bond that we never achieve in the church. They truly become like family.

They are able to sustain each other in community by stories sharing their lives with one another. When someone new joins the community, that person will learn some of the old stories that have sustained the community and will develop new stories as they become an integral part of the team. Certainly, firefighters have issues in their community like anyone else, but the analogy still illustrates how they are able to form a deeper sense of community than we often do in the church.

Wesley pushes us today toward a model of community that is transforming and takes our relationship with God and neighbor seriously. He challenges us to inward transformation that manifests in outward actions. An evangelistic community is a group of people who understand the journey does not end when we enter into the community; that is only the beginning.

Charles Wesley gives us words to meditate on concerning what it means to be a Christian community:

Jesus, Lord, we look to thee; let us in thy name agree; show thyself the Prince of Peace, bid our strife for ever cease.

By thy reconciling love every stumbling block remove; each to each unite, endear; come, and spread thy banner here.

Make us of one heart and mind, gentle, courteous, and kind, lowly meek, in thought and word, altogether like our Lord.

Let us for each other care, each the other's burdens bear; to the church the pattern give, show how true believers live.

Free from anger and from pride, let us thus in God abide; all the depths of love express, all the heights of holiness.

Let us then with joy remove to the family above; on the wings of angels fly, show how true believers die.[19]

Questions

1. Does your church understand itself to be an evangelistic community?

2. What attributes of an evangelistic community are currently a part of your church?

3. How can your church create a better balance between being an inviting community and a sustaining community?

4. What pattern of practices is your church developing to help people become more evangelistic?

5. What words or themes from Charles Wesley's hymn help you to better understand what it means to be in community?

# A God We Know

Beloved, let us love one another, because love is from God;
everyone who loves is born of God and knows God.
Whoever does not love does not know God, for God is love.
God's love was revealed among us in this way: God sent his
only Son into the world so that we might live through him.
In this is love, not that we loved God but that he loved us
and sent his Son to be the atoning sacrifice for our sins.
Beloved, since God loved us so much, we also ought to love
one another. No one has ever seen God; if we love one
another, God lives in us, and his love is perfected in us.

1 John 4:7-12

We saw in Chapter Two that evangelism in the Wesleyan tradition puts us on a journey in which we abide in Christ. Then in Chapter Three we saw how this evangelism is essentially relational, both in how it is practiced and in the salvation it promises. Drawing upon these points, we can now make a further one: Wesleyan evangelism helps us know God. What the good news promises is not just that we will know about God, though that is certainly important. What is promised is that we will know God through entering a relationship, and through that relationship will come to know that we belong to God.

To understand this point more clearly, it may be helpful to compare our knowledge of a public figure, such as a politician or celebrity, with our knowledge of a friend. We can know a lot about a public figure. We can read books written by researchers, as well as by their friends and critics. We can watch them on television or do a search on the internet. Over time we can compile quite a bit of information, some of which may help us understand them more accurately.

But we would never say we know them in the same way we know a friend. This is because we have a real, ongoing relationship with a friend. We spend time with them, converse with them directly, and over time come to know their personality and character in a way we never could of a public figure who was not also a friend. The relationship God wants to have with us is more like that with a friend, and is at the heart of the message of new life proclaimed in evangelism.

A relationship with God will not leave us unchanged. As it says in 1 John, it is those who know God that love one another, and only those who love can be said to know God and be born of God. So we are not only changed by entering into this relationship, we are changed in a particular way: we begin to love God and others as we have been loved by God.

There are two important ways a relationship with God is not like a relationship with another person. The first is that God is both our Creator and Redeemer, and as such is actively seeking to transform our lives so that they once again reflect the image of God in which we were created. The second is that a friend is physically present, while God's presence is not physical. Both of these aspects of a relationship with God—the power to live a new life and the presence of God in our lives—is the work of the Holy Spirit.

The problem with a presence that is not physical is that it makes it hard to sustain a relationship. This is why God has promised to be especially present through certain practices of worship and service called means of grace. It is in and through these very particular activities that we especially experience the presence of God.

The Means of Grace

Wesley identifies the means of grace as works of mercy and piety. Works of mercy are those actions of compassion and justice we do for our neighbor, and works of piety are those actions of worship and fellowship that are directed to God. (In Chapter Two we connected works of mercy and piety to the rules of discipline, a point we will return to in a moment.)

While no list is exhaustive, Wesley identifies five main works of piety: prayer, searching the Scriptures, the Lord's Supper, fasting, and Christian conversation. We can get a sense of how God uses these to maintain a relationship by thinking back to the analogy with a friend. To have a relationship with a friend, we have to be present to the friend, speaking, listening, doing things together, and sometimes just enjoying being with one another. Some of these works of piety—prayer, fasting, Christian conversation—seem especially designed to keep us open and attentive to God's presence in our lives.

Also in our relationship with a friend, we come to know the friend's personal characteristics and something of his or her story. This is what makes the friend who he or she is, and distinguishes that friend from other people we know. Some works of piety—searching the Scriptures, the Lord's Supper, and (again) prayer—seem especially designed to convey God's nature, purposes, promises, and all that God has done in creation and for our redemption.[1]

After all, God is not just whoever we think God is—God is revealed to us, distinctively in the history of Israel and definitively in Jesus Christ. This is why a daily devotional life and weekly worship is so crucial: it is where we again and again remember the story of God in Scripture and (in worship) participate in the Lord's Supper. Through these means of grace we encounter the God revealed in word and sacrament in a way that we experience who this God is.

It is as we study and listen to Scripture, give thanks and receive the bread and cup in the Lord's Supper, pray to God, put our need for God ahead of all other needs in fasting, and talk about the promises and purposes of God with other Christians, that the Holy Spirit works to transform our lives. As we encounter again and again God's unfailing and steadfast love in the means of grace, we grow in our love and knowledge of God.

It might seem strange for Wesley to claim that works of mercy are also means of grace. Certainly they may help us know our neighbor, but how do they help us know God? Yet many will testify how they visited someone in the hospital hoping to show how much they care, but found that they left feeling blessed themselves. If we engage in works of mercy, we find we grow in our compassion and insight. We may learn to receive as well as to give. We begin to see things a bit more from God's perspective, and in so doing come to know God's love more deeply. The Holy Spirit, then, not only works through us to minister to others, but through others to help us grow in our Christian life.

None of this means we have salvation without faith. The doing of works of piety and mercy do not earn us points with God, but are means through which we relate to God. But they are only means of grace for us if we come to them with a degree of faith. Faith is how we know God, so to participate in means of grace with faith is to open ourselves to experience God's presence in them. Note that faith does not cause God to be present, but it discerns the reality of God in the means of grace.

Now we can see why it was so vital for Methodist evangelism to result in persons joining a class and committing to a discipline. First, it ensured a regular participation in both works of mercy and works of piety. Second, by countering dissipation, it nurtured the faith necessary to know the presence of God in the means of grace. Together, this opened persons to a transforming encounter with God, enabling them to receive and grow in new life.

Knowing We Belong to God

In addition to knowing God, Wesleyan evangelism also promises that we can know we are accepted by God. The classic example comes from John Wesley himself. While attending a meeting on Aldersgate Street in London, Wesley heard the words of Martin Luther's Preface to his commentary on Paul's letter to the Romans. Here is what happened, in Wesley's own words:

> About a quarter before nine, while he [Luther] was describing the change which God works in the heart through faith in Christ, I felt my heart strangely warmed. I felt I did trust in Christ, Christ alone for salvation; and an assurance was given me that he had taken away *my* sins, even *mine*, and saved *me* from the law of sin and death.[2]

In this event Wesley received the faith of a child of God ("I felt I did trust in Christ . . ."), experienced justification ("he had taken away my sins . . ."), and did so in such a way that he knew he was reconciled by God (". . . an assurance was given me . . .").

What Wesley means by an assurance here he will later call the witness of the Spirit. This he defines as "an inward impression on the soul, whereby the Spirit of God directly 'witnesses to my spirit that I am a child of God;' that Jesus Christ hath loved me, and given himself for me; that all my sins are blotted out, and I, even I, am reconciled to God."[3] Wesley himself says that it is hard to find words to describe this witness. But it is clear he is not speaking of a particular set of feelings, such as having a warm heart, but of an inner conviction or confidence that one has been forgiven and reconciled.

There are three things that need to be said about this assurance. First, Wesley maintains an emphasis on *God* as the one who forgives, reconciles, and transforms. Some forms of evangelism urge persons to "accept Christ." Certainly Wesleyan evangelism would urge people to come to Christ, or to enter into a relationship with God through Christ. But it is more apt to ask if we have come to know we are accepted by Christ than to ask whether we have accepted Christ. This assurance is *given* to us. Our response to God is important, but much more important is what God does.

Second, the witness of the Spirit must be held in balance with the "witness of our own spirit." This is an "indirect witness" whereby a person is conscious of having the fruits of the Spirit as described in Scripture, and from that concludes he or she is a child of God.[4] If one has been truly born into a new life, the fruits will be present (". . . everyone who loves is born of God and knows God." 1 John 4:7). From this Wesley infers that there can be no witness of the Spirit separate from the fruits of the Spirit.[5] Those who say they had a powerful conversion experience or that they know they have salvation, but whose hearts and lives do not manifest at least the beginnings of faith, hope, and love, are deceiving themselves. Salvation is especially witnessed by how we treat others ("Whoever does not love does not know God . . ." 1 John 4:8). Of course, the Christian life involves growing in love and the other fruit of the Spirit. But salvation means we have actually begun that journey, we are actually living that new life. No inner conviction of acceptance by God is credible if there is not at the same time a transformed life.

Third, salvation is through trusting in Jesus Christ, not in having an assurance. While Wesley believed the witness of the Spirit normally accompanied justification and the new birth, he abandoned his early belief that it always does so. We are saved by faith, alone. There are those who show the fruit of the new life but have not experienced an inward sense of acceptance. Yet Wesley believes to have this assurance "is the privilege of a child of God."[6] Moreover, it is important to our steady growth as Christians. He therefore urges those who have the fruit of the Spirit but not the witness of the Spirit to cry out to God until they know they are children of God.

Charles Wesley gives us words to pray both for the faith that enables us to know God, and for the assurance that we belong to God:

> Spirit of faith, come down, reveal the things of God,
> and make to us the God-head known, and witness
> with the blood.
> 'Tis thine the blood to apply and give us eyes to see,
> who did for every sinner die hath surely
> died for me.

Inspire the living faith (which whosoever receive,
  the witness in themselves they have and
    consciously believe),
the faith that conquers all, and doth the mountain move
  and saves whoe'er on Jesus call,
  and perfects them in love.[7]

Questions

1. How would you compare knowing about God with knowing God? How are each important to the Christian life?

2. How can evangelism be practiced to invite or encourage persons to have a relationship with God?

3. How do the various works of piety contribute to our knowing God? How do works of mercy contribute?

4. How can we know we are children of God?

A Word We Proclaim

In the beginning was the Word, and the Word was with
God, and the Word was God. He was in the beginning
with God. All things came into being through him, and
without him not one thing came into being. What has
come into being in him was life, and the life was the light
of all people. The light shines in the darkness and the
darkness did not overcome it. John 1:1-5

In the last chapter we talked about how it is that we can know
God. Being evangelistic requires more than just knowledge
about God, it requires proclaiming the good news of the gospel.
Many Christians are comfortable learning about Jesus the Christ,
but are uncomfortable testifying about Jesus. In our postmodern
society, many argue what one believes is personal and not open to
public scrutiny. The idea of intentionally testifying or sharing one's
faith is frightening in our society and foreign to many Christians
today. Being evangelistic by word and deed means a willingness to
risk an openness to others we may find uncomfortable.

Wesley took this risk when he shared his Aldersgate experience
with others by writing it in his journal on May 24, 1738:

In the evening I went very unwillingly to a society in Aldersgate-Street, where one was reading Luther's preface to the Epistle to the Romans. About a quarter before nine, while he was describing the change which God works in the heart through faith in Christ, I felt my heart strangely warmed. I felt I did trust in Christ, Christ alone for salvation; and an assurance was given me, that he had taken away *my* sins, even *mine*, and saved *me* from the law of sin and death.[1]

The risk of proclaiming God's word is at the heart of evangelism. God works in all of our lives and we are called to testify to others about God's actions. Wesley did just that in the above passage telling others how his heart was strangely warmed that night in 1738. Yet, one of the reasons the above testimony by Wesley is so debated today is our personal encounters with the gospel are often taken as the lens through which others should encounter God. Even Wesley in looking back on this experience did not perceive it as "the one experience" of encountering God in his life. Our encounters with the gospel are ongoing, meaning we create new testimonies all the time. An evangelistic lesson from Wesley's Aldersgate experience is thinking about the importance of the gospel intersecting with our lives enabling us to testify to God's transforming power. Wesley's Aldersgate experience makes for a powerful testimony because you can picture the word becoming flesh as he describes the scene

Proclaiming God's word does not necessarily mean preaching the gospel as a professional. Wesley did not believe it was only the preachers' job to proclaim the message or to testify. One of the strengths of the Wesleyan revival was that it involved the laity in sharing the good news of the gospel. The notion in some congregations that the preacher alone is responsible for evangelism would not be consistent with our Wesleyan tradition. All Christians are called to play a role in testifying to the good news of the gospel. The preacher plays a particular role in preaching sermons and teaching, but that does not exclude the responsibility of all believers from playing a role in spreading the good news.

The Word Made Flesh[2]

John 1:1-5 gives a description of how the Word became flesh. It is a powerful description because it creates a vivid picture bringing the gospel to life. Wesley was able to bring the gospel to life in his revival and to put "flesh on the word." The incarnation of Jesus as the Word is unique because God enters the world. Our putting flesh on the gospel is contextualizing—bringing the good news to where people can understand it. Yet, our contextualizing the gospel is not the same as the incarnation of Christ. For us, it is because of the incarnation of Christ that we are able to put flesh on the word—make the gospel come alive. At this juncture we will highlight three ways Wesley was able to put flesh on the word in his revival.

WESLEY TOOK THE WORD TO THE PEOPLE

Taking the word to the people is not always easy and even Wesley had reservations at first. Wesley was ordained into a high church tradition as a clergyperson in the Church of England. By high church we mean the emphasis placed on liturgy and a proper way of conducting church. The problem with conducting church in a certain manner is it only appealed to a certain percentage of the population. George Whitefield, seeing the church was not reaching everyone, started preaching in the fields to common workers and any who would come. He invited Wesley to do the same and to reach out to a different audience.

Wesley describes his reservations about preaching outside of the Church of England in the fields:

> I could scarce reconcile myself at first to this 'strange way' of preaching in the fields, of which he set me an example on Sunday; having been all my life (till very lately) so tenacious of every point relating to decency and order, that I should have thought the saving of souls 'almost a sin,' if it had not been done in a church.[3]

A telling lesson for us today from Wesley's experience is our reservations about sharing the gospel in different circumstances. Initially, Wesley did not believe a person could be saved outside of the church walls and devalued the effect preaching in the fields would have on people. We are not suggesting people today need to go stand in a field and preach, but taking the word outside of the church walls is still relevant today. Once Wesley began preaching outside of the church walls he discovered the power of taking the word to the people.

As Wesley embraced field preaching he began to see the word of God reaching audiences who never attended church. Wesley remarks in his journal on Sunday, September 23, 1759 are very different from those he made twenty years early during his initial experience:

> A vast majority of the immense congregation in Moorfields were deeply serious. One such hour might convince any impartial man of the expediency of "field-preaching." What building, except St. Paul's church, would contain such a congregation?

And if it would, what human voice could have reached them there? By repeated observations I find I can command thrice the number in the open air, that I can under a roof. And who can say the time for field-preaching is over, while, 1. Greater numbers than ever attend: 2. The converting, as well as convincing, power of God is eminently present with them?[4]

In the twenty years between 1739 and 1759, Wesley came to realize that taking the word to the people was just as powerful and in some cases more powerful than waiting for the people to come hear the word. Wesley's second point above that the "converting, as well as convincing, power of God is eminently present"[5] with the people reinforces the notion of God working outside of the confines of the church building. Like Wesley in 1739, too many of us today believe people should come to our building to hear the word of God. Thinking evangelistically means the willingness to take the word of God to the people.

During Wesley's day preaching in the field was culturally relevant and a way to take the word to the people. Certainly, in this age of multiple media options the good news is spread throughout the airwaves to millions already. Yet, many of the media approaches today miss the personal contact that Wesley had with those who came to hear him preach. He did not preach just for conversions or simply to attract large crowds. Wesley believed the word of God would make a difference in the lives of those who came and would continue to make a difference in their lives if they started a journey toward the recovery of the image of God.

Field preaching was not an end for Wesley, in the sense that he was strictly concerned with going from city to city to preach. Field preaching was a means for getting the word of God out to those who did not come to church and letting them know God accepted them. Wesley made the word come alive and become flesh for many who had not heard the gospel in this manner. Evangelism requires making the word come alive, it requires making the Word a reality to those who are still seeking forgiveness and acceptance.

Wesley comments on the importance of taking the word to the people in his journal:

> About seven I preached at the Gins, and the people flocked together from all quarters. The want of field-preaching has been one cause of deadness here. I do not find any great increase of the work of God without it. If ever this is laid aside, I expect the whole work will gradually die away.[6]

We would be wise to hear Wesley's words today not to become "dead" by sitting on the word of God. We must find ways to carry the word outside of the church in culturally relevant ways so that we do not "gradually die away."

WESLEY MADE THE WORD RELEVANT TO THEIR LIVES

Helping people see the word become flesh requires making it relevant to their situation. Wesley was able to do this in a variety of ways in the Methodist revival. Some credit in this case, however, should be given to Charles Wesley and the impact of his hymns. Charles was able to capture in melody the theology that under-girded the revival. He was able to make a connection with the people enabling them to make the hymns their own. The Wesleys were able to establish some common ground with those in the revival through the singing of the hymns.

For example, those needing words to express God's forgiveness and acceptance could relate to Charles' hymn, "'Tis Finished! The Messiah Dies:"

'Tis finished! All my guilt and pain,
I want no sacrifice beside;
for me, for me the Lamb is slain;
'Tis finished! I am justified.

The reign of sin and death is o'er and
All may live from sin set free;
Satan hath lost his mortal power;
'tis swallowed up in victory.[7]

Charles Wesley was able to put into music the words that would help people to relate to Jesus' act of reconciling us to God—enabling us to be forgiven and accepted. The ability of Charles to take the theological concepts essential to the movement and to make them accessible by music cannot be understated. An example some can relate to from the sixties is the importance of music to the Civil Rights Movement. The song "We Shall Overcome" put into melody the theme of the movement in a way that was accessible to all involved. A more recent example comes from the tragedy of 9/11. Many people found hymns to be meaningful in a way they were not before, conveying the strength and the hope of the country.

The point is music has the ability to convey a message in a way that other forms of transmission do not. The Wesleys understood the importance of music and it helped them to be culturally relevant to those in the movement. The challenge today is writing music with the theological depth of Charles Wesley that remains culturally relevant to the people. This does not mean replacing the Wesley hymns, but it does mean finding new ways to express the theological depth of Charles' hymns for a new generation. Kenneth Carter makes a similar suggestion that is worth exploring.

He writes,

> Despite John Wesley's insistence that one should "learn these tunes before you learn any others; afterwards learn as many as you please," our singing is sometimes shaped by other streams of Christian tradition, from revivalist gospel to contemporary praise to social gospel, music that does not always possess the depth of doctrinal richness found in the writings of Charles Wesley. Some of the hymn supplements and songbooks of the last century included almost none of the Wesley hymns, and many congregations that have transitioned from traditional to contemporary forms of worship have lost touch with this practice as well. I am not suggesting a blanket indictment on non-Wesleyan hymns or praise choruses; I am simply suggesting that we test newer resources for worship in light of the music that has shaped our tradition for 250 years.[8]

Carter's observation is well warranted, but we must be careful not to get trapped into using resources people do not understand or cannot relate to currently. His point, however, about testing the newer resources is a good one if our goal is theological depth. Being evangelistic within the Wesleyan tradition means maintaining the theological moorings so essential to the Wesleys, while maintaining a cultural relevance to today's society. Charles was able to do so with his music and it made a difference evangelistically for the movement. We must find ways to do so today or we run the risk on one side of theological shallowness and on the other side of cultural irrelevance. Music is a powerful medium for evangelism, but it is a medium that needs to navigate between theological depth and cultural relevance.

The second way Wesley made the word relevant to the people was his holistic approach. Evangelism within the Wesleyan tradition takes into consideration the entire person and not simply saving the soul while ignoring the body. Wesley was able to relate to those in the field he was preaching to because he was concerned with their spiritual and physical well-being. He wrote a book on common remedies, *Primitive Physik*, to help those who could not afford a doctor. He started Kingswood school to educate the children of those less fortunate. These types of actions made the gospel come alive in a different way for many people who had not experienced a holistic approach to the word.

The key word for what Wesley did is relational. Wesley made the gospel relevant by making it relational and not something done to people. It is one thing to be told God forgives and accepts you and never to experience that forgiveness and acceptance from others in the community. Wesley encouraged people to live out in holistic ways the forgiveness and acceptance of God. To do this requires relating to others in a way that some had not experienced previously and certainly not experienced in connection to the gospel.

In the church today we must work hard to make the gospel relevant by taking a holistic approach like Wesley. Evangelism means developing relationships with people and bringing them into a different type of community. Striving towards holiness is another way of talking about striving toward wholeness within the Wesley tradition. In a society where we frequently experience brokenness because of split families, unfulfilling careers, financial hardships, etc., Wesley's emphasis on holiness is still relevant and a message we must proclaim. Some may be disappointed that holiness does not mean life will be defined on their terms, but it does mean a life participating with God. This life is lived differently because we are no longer held captive by the brokenness that so often defines our being.

Interestingly, one of the first sermons (April 2, 1739) Wesley preached in the fields was the Luke 4:18 text:

> The Spirit of the Lord is upon me,
> because he has anointed me
> to bring good news to the poor.
> He has sent me to proclaim
> release to the captives
> and recovery of sight to the blind,
> to let the oppressed go free,
> to proclaim the year of the
> Lord's favor. (Luke 4:18)

Wesley's choice of the Lukan passage is a foreshadowing of things to come in his ministry. The Luke passage speaks to forms of brokenness people experience in life and the fact that the Lord has good news for these individuals. Wesley brought the good news of holiness to many who had not heard this word before. His evangelistic message was relevant to many during his day and is still relevant today because it reminds us that we can move toward wholeness in this life.

WESLEY ENCOURAGED PARTICIPATION

Wesley encouraged the laity to participate in the process of salvation, meaning salvation was not something done to you, but it was something done with you. God's transformation is possible because humans participate with God in the process. In thinking about evangelism this is important because the laity must play an active role concerning evangelism. As organized and charismatic as Wesley was the Methodist Movement would not have been a success without the participation of many.

A radical example in Wesley's day was his enabling women in the movement to participate more fully in ministry. In his sermon, "On Visiting the Sick," Wesley argues for women to play a stronger role in ministry:

> Let all you (women) that have in your power assert the right which the God of nature has given you. Yield not to that vile bondage any longer! You, as well as men, are rational creatures. You, like them, were made in the image of God; you are equally candidates for immortality. You too are called of God, as you have time, to "do good unto all men." Be "not disobedient to the heavenly calling." Whenever you have opportunity, do all the good you can, particularly to your poor, sick neighbour.[9]

Being proactive, Wesley went even further encouraging some women to become the leaders of classes and bands.[10] From an evangelistic perspective what we do not want to lose is Wesley giving voice to the women. We can only speculate, but it is not a stretch to believe for the women who participated in the Methodist movement the word did take on flesh in a different way because of their active participation. The women involved in the movement were able to give voice to what Jesus meant to them and not just relate to it second hand through a man.

In his journal Wesley retells the last days of Lydia Vandome and her service in ministry to the gospel:

> On Tuesday evening last, she desired us to set her up in bed, to meet her class. Her voice faltered much. She earnestly exhorted them all to live near to God, and to keep close together; adding, 'I shall soon join the church above.' She spoke no more; all was silent rapture, til, on Friday morning, without sigh or groan, she resigned her spirit to God.[11]

The church today can learn from Wesley the importance of giving voice to everyone in the congregation. If we all are active participants with God in the process of salvation, then we all should have a voice in testifying about the process. One person or committee cannot be responsible for doing evangelism for the entire church. The laity need to be active in testifying about what God is doing in their lives. Wesley was able to encourage active participation in his movement by giving voice to the people. The word really becomes flesh when we consciously participate in God's transforming work and not just sit back as non-interested bystanders.

This notion of not being a bystander also is true for worship. Specifically, Wesley encouraged the People Called Methodists to participate in communion as frequently as possible. One of the purposes of communion is the celebration of Jesus' resurrection which symbolizes the possibility of new life for all believers. Participating in communion is one of the most profound ways to experience the Word becoming flesh. It was the presence of Jesus the Christ in this meal that had such a huge impact on the early Methodist:

> The desire of the early Methodists to receive the Lord's Supper as often as possible is well known. The enormous crowds of communicants would sometimes take hours to serve. Why this hunger for the sacrament? They were convinced that, through the power of the Holy Spirit, the risen Jesus Christ was present in this meal, and by receiving his gift of bread and wine, they would be given new life. They came with an expectant faith, seeking to remember all that God has done and promised through Jesus Christ and open to receive all God has to give.[12]

There may be no better way to celebrate the Word becoming flesh than in communion with each other. This is not a perfunctory act, but one that has deep meaning for our Christian lives together. Remembering what Jesus did by dying and rising from the dead reminds us of God's acceptance and the promise of new life. We are called to share with others that God accepts them too. The promise of living as new people means we must continue to strive together as a community, encouraging each other in the faith.

Wesley encouraged participation at different levels within the revival. Like Wesley, we must encourage laity today to actively participate in the transforming work of God. We must give voice to everyone so they can consciously take ownership of the word. We must remember what Jesus did for us as we look forward to living as new people. Participation means the laity are involved in proclaiming the word and need not to shy away from testifying to how God is working in their life.

Testimony

We have outlined some ways Wesley made the word to become flesh in his context and what this means for us today evangelistically. It is by participation, especially by the laity, that the word begins to come alive. Unfortunately, many churches struggle to get laity involved in the ministry of evangelism. The word "evangelism" at times almost seems like a curse word in the church. There is a story about a lady who went weekly to a nursing home and taught a sewing and Bible study class. Her class at the nursing home was successful so the pastor wanted her to be a part of the evangelism committee. She was horrified that the pastor would suggest such a thing—it was as if she had insulted her. The pastor pointed out she was already engaging in evangelism at the nursing home. She denied any such action and explained she was only sharing her gift of sewing with a few favorite Bible verses.

Helping laity not react so negatively to the word evangelism is important if the church is going to get more people involved in this ministry. The lady in the story above was sharing the gospel at the nursing home, but she was afraid of the term evangelism. One way to think about what we hope people will do in sharing the gospel is to talk about testimonies.

Many terms are used to describe the act of sharing one's faith: sharing, faith-sharing, witnessing, testifying, and of course evangelizing. We will focus on the term testimony because it is a term that has some history within the Wesleyan revival. Testimonies were an integral part of the love feast services. It was an opportunity for participants to share openly with others what God was doing in their life.

Frank Baker, a leading historian of early Methodism, comments about the love feast:

> Scores of references to love feasts in eighteenth- and nineteenth-century diaries and journals testify to the fact that though the common meal was of real importance as a symbol of Christian family life, and though prayer and singing were inseparable from such occasions, the focal point was testimony, the spiritual 'sharing' to which the taking of food and drink together was the symbolic prelude.[13]

Baker's intention is not to play down the role of the meal itself, but to highlight the importance of testimony to the Methodist revival. It was an essential component of the love feast that allowed participants to share what God was doing in their lives. The term testimony, however, has baggage dating back to the revival because it is often used strictly in conjunction with people telling about their conversion experience. This is one of the problems with Wesley's Aldersgate experience if it is perceived as his "one" testimonial experience. The term testimony is richer than just stories about conversions; it is a term that describes the intersection between our story and the gospel story. What we testify to as believers is that intersection and how it has transformed or is transforming our lives. Testimony is about what God is doing in our lives and sharing that experience with others.

Varieties of Testimony

Prayer Service

Prayer service or testimonial service is one type of testimony. The prayer service in America is closely connected to the love feast service practiced by the early Methodist. In general there is a time of testifying, singing, and praying. In these services people would talk about their conversion experiences, different "tests" God helped them to get through or just proclaim the goodness of God. There are two points we will highlight related to evangelism that are central to these type of services.

First, one of the strengths of this type of service is it is interactive and helped people to gain the courage to speak openly about their faith. In making the word become flesh we discussed the importance of participation. What Wesley writes about a love feast is also applicable to a prayer service, "Many were surprised when I told them 'The very design of a love-feast is a free and familiar conversation . . .'"[14] This style of a prayer service is predicated on participation and encourages people to share their story, giving them the confidence to do so outside of the service.

The prayer service is not as common today in our churches. Yet, we come together often for different committee meetings and Bible studies. Encouraging a few people to share what God is doing in their lives during these meetings is one way to reclaim the essence of "free and familiar conversation." The hope is to help people to become comfortable in talking about the transformation God is doing in their lives. By practicing their testimony with those hopefully sympathetic to them it will give them the confidence to share with others they may be in relationship with outside of the church.

Second, the prayer service is about listening and a willingness to hear the story of someone else. Listening is one of the toughest skills to develop. Many of us can hardly wait until someone else is done talking so we can get our point across. At the prayer services the ability to hear the stories of others was just as important as telling your own story. Jesus listened to others and heard their voices. For example, in Matthew 20:31-33, two blind men in a crowd were yelling for Jesus to have mercy upon them. The crowd tried to quiet them, but Jesus heard their voices and healed them. An integral part of testimony is the ability to hear the voice of another.

It is not uncommon for some of us to drift in and out of a conversation when someone is talking with us. Our lives are hectic and we are constantly looking forward to the next thing we must get done. One of the secrets of evangelism is not necessarily having a silver tongue, but having open ears. The willingness to sit and listen to someone tell their story can be just as compelling as telling your own story. Prayer services encouraged people to listen and be able to hear the stories of others.

COMMUNAL TESTIMONY

In the African-American Church tradition the testimony is often in the words to a song. The intersection between stories (personal and gospel) is sung and the message of transformation was clear to those who were singing.

One such song is "Freedom Train a-comin:"

> Hear that-a freedom train a coming,
> Coming, coming, Hear that freedom
> Train a coming, coming, coming, Hear
> That freedom train a coming, coming, coming,
> Get on board, oh,_____ oh, get on board.[15]

This was a song usually sung in the South during the Civil Rights Movement to let people know that help was on the way. The idea behind the song is God will help those currently suffering just like he helped Daniel out of the lion's den or the three Hebrew boys out of the fiery furnace. The song is a testimony that illuminates the intersection between the story of the African-American people suffering in the South and the fact that God's help is on the way. The song is transformative because the community has experienced God's help in the past and the expectation is it will experience it again in the future.

This form of communal testimony is evangelistic because the songs reach a broad audience made up of believers and seekers. A communal testimony is not meant to instantaneously make one a believer, but is a way of sharing how God is working in the community. For believers the power of communal testimonies is to create reference points for the community as a whole to talk about God's actions. One of the communal markers for the Israelite's was the crossing of the Red Sea and their freedom from the

Egyptians. For seekers it is a way of accessing how God has worked in the community and how God has transformed the community. The hope is that seekers will begin to see themselves as a part of the on-going story as the community creates new testimonies concerning God's actions.

Churches can develop these communal testimonies that can help old and new members to understand God's workings in their midst. Many churches have stories concerning acts of kindness in the community, justice stances or even the survival of the church during an especially tough time. These communal testimonies are important in helping new members to understand the role God has played in the community and they remind the older members of God's actions. Keeping alive communal testimonies is important evangelistically as churches seek to integrate new and old members together.

PRAISE REPORTS AND PRAYER REQUESTS

A more common form of testimony used by churches today is often called praise reports and prayer requests. Some churches will allow time during the actual worship service for these reports and requests. Other churches will use other mechanisms like prayer boxes, cards, etc., to give people a chance to express themselves. The actual testimony usually comes in the praise report, but the prayer requests component is important because often the praise report is a result of an answered prayer.

One of the advantages for taking time during the worship service for praise reports and prayer requests is the community gets to hear the person making the report or the requests. If there are visitors in the congregation it allows them to eavesdrop in on what is going on with people in the congregation. The challenge to allowing time during a worship service for praise reports and prayer requests is some individuals can be long-winded and the pastor usually has no clue what someone will say. To counter the first challenge, it is good to encourage people to speak only for two minutes.

Countering the second challenge is more difficult because you want to encourage the testimonies and the prayer requests. Yet it is important for people to be sensitive to others when they are speaking. Helping people understand that you do not have to stand every week to report your son scored a touchdown in the football game or your daughter scored a goal in soccer is tricky, but necessary. Achievements by people in the congregation are important and a time needs to be put aside to acknowledge their accomplishments. The praise reports and prayer requests time, however, is usually not that time.

The goal is to speak to the intersection between our story and the gospel story. A sports accomplishment or doing well on a test, etc., are important, but we need to be careful that God does not become our personal Santa Claus granting our wishes. The other danger is implying God is somehow blessing "me" and not others. The power in the praise reports is others can hear and sometimes see the intersection between the stories and how God's transformation is at work in the intersection.

Wesley writes about a love feast at Burslem where he hints at the power of God's transforming work through the testimonies of others:

> The love-feast followed, but such a one as I have not known for many years. While the two or three first spoke, the power of God so fell upon all that were present, some praying, and others giving thanks, that their voices could scarce be heard. And two or three were speaking at a time, till I gently advised them to speak one at a time, and they did so with amazing energy.[16]

A praise report can be a powerful testimony to what God is doing in someone's life. As Wesley reports it can help others to experience the power of God through the testimony. Praise reports are an important evangelistic expression if done thoughtfully and sensitively. It is a way to encourage people to share their story before others in a caring atmosphere. The goal is to get laity involved through encouraging them to talk about what they know, not to create fear by telling them they must share in a certain manner.

We have offered three varieties of testimony above (prayer service, communal testimonies, and praise reports and prayer requests) that are options for congregations looking to proclaim the good news. All three encourage people to discuss the intersection between their story and the gospel story. All three point to God's transforming work as the real impetus in evangelizing.

What is unique about this approach? There is nothing new or unique about this approach. It is an attempt to reclaim the active participation by laity today in evangelism that seemed prevalent during Wesley's revival. During Wesley's time the people were not professional evangelists with special training. Many of the early Methodists were not scholars or individuals who went to school for ministry. They were people who were willing to share what God was doing in their lives to transform them. Are we willing to do the same?

Wesley writes about some of the individuals who were a part of the revival:

> I have seldom heard people speak with more honesty and simplicity than many did at the love-feast which followed. I have not seen a more unpolished people than these; but love supplies all defects. It supplies all the essentials of good breeding, without the help of a dancing-master.[17]

74

A Lesson for Today

We should learn from Wesley that it is not necessary to be a professional evangelist. The truth is professional evangelists turn many of us off. We live in a society where a testimony from our friend carries as much weight as one from a so-called professional. For example, in buying a car many of us will ask our friends what they like and dislike about their vehicle. We trust what they are telling us to be true and will often make a decision based upon their testimony. We should not think it is our job to bring someone to a decision through our testimonies, but we can tell them the truth about our experience with the gospel. We can make the word become flesh for them by telling what God is doing in our life.

Charles Wesley helps us to think about the power of our tongues and how they can make the word flesh in his hymn, "O For a Thousand Tongues to Sing:"

O for a thousand tongues to sing my great Redeemers's praise,
the glories of my God and King, the triumphs of his grace!

My gracious Master and my God, assist me to proclaim,
to spread through all the earth abroad the honors of thy name.

Jesus! the name that charms our fears, that bids our sorrows
cease;
'tis music in the sinner's ears, 'tis life, and health and peace.

He breaks the power of canceled sin, he sets the prisoner free;
his blood can make the foulest clean; his blood availed for me.

He speaks and listening to his voice, new life the dead receive;
The mournful broken hearts rejoice, the humble poor believe.

Hear him, ye deaf; his praise, ye dumb, your loosened tongues
   employ;
ye blind, behold your Savior come, and leap, ye lame, for joy.

In Christ, your head, you then shall know shall feel your sins forgiven;
anticipate your heaven below, and own that love is heaven.[18]

In our society today, Charles may think we need even more
tongues—even your tongue—to testify about Jesus' glory throughout all the earth. He would certainly believe we should proclaim the
good news and not be afraid to talk about God's transforming work
in our lives.

Questions

1. Does your congregation think it is only the pastor's job to
   spread the good news?

2. Can you describe a time when the word was made flesh in
   your life?

3. What would taking the word outside of your church require?

4. How can people become more active in worship?

5. Where has your story intersected with the gospel story?

6. How does Charles Wesley's hymn "O For a Thousand
   Tongues to Sing" help you to think about the importance of
   testimony?

THE WESLEYAN WAY OF EVANGELISM

He said to him, "'You shall love the Lord your God with
all your heart, and with all your soul, and with your mind.'
This is the greatest and first commandment. And a second
is like it: 'You shall love your neighbor as yourself.'
Matthew 22:37-39

In the first chapter we defined evangelism within the Wesleyan tradition as: *Our sharing and inviting others to experience the good news that God loves us and invites us into a transforming relationship through which we are forgiven, receive new life, and are restored to the image of God, which is love.* What this definition and the preceding chapters convey is that, for Wesley, evangelism is about relationship: how we are in relationship to God, who is able to transform us into new beings; how we are in relationship to our neighbor, whom we must love like ourselves.

Scott Jones, a former professor of evangelism and current bishop, explains what this relationship to God and neighbor means:

Taking all three Gospel versions together, loving God with everything one has and loving one's neighbor as oneself has a kind of
priority and centrality to God's will for humanity that is of the

highest order. All other duties flow from and are subordinate to these two commands. Since "love" is a relational word, this involves the kind of response that the rest of the New Testament describes as faith. In so doing, they are to love all those whom God loves. Called "the neighbor" in the Leviticus text, the other whom we are to love is an all-inclusive other.[1]

The "priority" of loving God and neighbor defines what it is God expects from Christians. Our loving God must intersect with loving our neighbor. The challenge in evangelism is not making this intersection cheap or controlling. By cheap, we mean the tendency at times for some of us to put limits on who is our neighbor. We sometimes define our neighbor in such a way that the neighbor really is just a reflection of ourselves. This is cheap love because the Bible calls for us to define our neighbor in the broadest sense.

The story of the "Good Samaritan" in Luke is an example of cheap love. The lawyer knew the two central commandments about love, but the lawyer wanted to restrict who was his neighbor. Jesus challenged the lawyer and challenges us to broaden who it is we think is our neighbor. In evangelism if we only seek to love those who are like us, then we cheapen God's call to love all who are our neighbor. One of the challenges of evangelism is broadening who is our neighbor and the responsibility we have towards them.

Another challenge in evangelism is attempting to make "my gospel" the supreme way the gospel should be understood. This is trying to not only control the gospel, but others through the gospel. For example, consider Wesley's hesitation to engage in field preaching—discussed in Chapter Five—because he initially did not believe salvation was possible outside of the walls of the church. His reluctance at first to preach in the field was an effort to control the way the gospel was spread to others. When we begin determining who should receive the gospel and how they should receive it, then we are trying to control what it means to love our neighbor. It is no longer a love based upon God's agenda, but an agenda we have created.

Both of these challenges to loving God and neighbor are important to point out in talking about the centrality of relationships to evangelism. It is easy to move to one extreme or the other in the name of evangelism. A more contemporary example of cheap love is a congregation reluctant to integrate the ethnically different youth from the neighborhood into their youth group. In this time of drive-in churches it is easy to ignore evangelizing and loving those directly in the neighborhood. Similarly, a contemporary example that highlights controlling love is the unwillingness of some churches to allow youth a voice in worship. If worship is not presented exactly as some "authority figures" design it, then it cannot be worship.

The Wesleyan way of evangelism seeks to navigate between the extremes of cheap love and controlling love in the way we live out the intersection between loving God and neighbor. It recognizes God's love and grace can operate in various ways depending on the circumstances. Our job is to help others to experience that love, and we do this by becoming aware of the needs of others.

Thus, the Wesleyan way of evangelism takes seriously the needs of others, whether those needs are physical or spiritual. How we are in relationship with others in meeting those needs, however, may differ given the circumstances. The Wesleyan way always keeps in mind the challenges we face in loving others while recognizing it is only by loving others that God's love can be expressed in concrete ways. Thus for Wesley, loving God and our neighbor is not a component of evangelism, it is what governs our practice of evangelism.

Love of God and of Neighbor

Wesley writes that "a Methodist is one who has 'the love of God shed abroad in his heart by the Holy Ghost given unto him . . . .'"[2] Wesley, of course, would claim that having this love shed abroad in one's heart will manifest itself in love for one's neighbor. In thinking about loving God and neighbor within the Wesleyan tradition we will highlight three ideas consistent with this theme.

REFLECTING IT TO OTHERS

The notion of reflecting God's love to others is not original with Wesley. It is especially prevalent within the Eastern Orthodox tradition of the church. Theologian Theodore Runyon, drawing on Wesley's sermon, "The Image of God," describes how Wesley understood this:

> Wesley . . . sees the image more relationally, not so much as something humans possess as the way they relate to God and live out that relation in the world. Thus in an early sermon he describes human beings as receiving the love of God and then *reflecting* that love toward all creatures. Not image as a human capability or inherent possession, but as a living relationship called forth by divine grace.[3]

Runyon illustrates this reflecting of God's love with the metaphor of a mirror, which he borrows from the Eastern tradition. His point is humans are to mirror God in their own lives and to reflect God's love to others.[4] Reflecting God's love is therefore a process with two steps. The first is us mirroring what it means to love God. The second is humanity reflecting God's love to others, becoming a "mirror" for them to see God. Evangelistically this has ramifications for us as individuals and as a community of faith.

As individuals we have to be renewed in the image of God so that we can reflect it to others. Wesley talked about this renewal in various ways throughout his life, such as our having the mind of Christ.

Wesley writes,

> Set your heart firm on him, and on other things only as they are in and from him. 'Let your soul be filled with so entire a love of him that you may love nothing but for his sake.' 'Have a pure intention of heart, a steadfeast regard to his glory in all your actions.' 'Fix your eye upon the blessed hope of your calling, and make all the things of the world minister unto it.' For then, and not till then, is that 'mind in us which was also in Christ Jesus', when in every motion of our heart, in every word of our tongue in every work of our hands, we 'pursue nothing but in relation to him, and in subordination to his pleasure . . . .'[5]

A heart firmly set on having the mind of Christ is the way for us to recover the image of God in order to reflect it to others. Notice Wesley's admonition in the sermon above that our words and actions should be pursued in relation to Christ. Evangelistically this means we must learn to honestly reflect the love and compassion of Christ and not attempt to manipulate others in the name of Christ. Scaring people into loving Christ is not what Wesley means by loving God with one's whole heart and our neighbor as ourselves. Wesley believes we should delight in God and continually rejoice in God's will—this is true love.[6] This is what Christians are called to reflect to others at all times, but especially when evangelizing.

Reflecting the image of God not only has ramifications for individuals, but also for the community. In Chapter Three we talked about inviting communities and the importance of the community being open to others as they seek Christ. One of the important ways a community is inviting is being hospitable to others. Reflecting the love of Christ as a community means others should not feel like strangers among us.

Shirley Clement and Roger Swanson, who have written on how our congregations can be genuinely welcoming, describe loving hospitality this way:

> In your congregation are strangers offered the hospitality of home? Think about the experience of being a member of your congregation. For many people church is the one place, other than the family, where they experience the warmth of being welcomed home. People there know you and you know them, or at least a significant number of them. They are glad to see you, as you are glad to see them. You exchange news, catch up with each other's lives, support each other in common tasks and in times of need. The essence of hospitality is to be known and welcomed, needed and loved.[7]

It sounds very cliché, but the theme song to the show Cheers, "you want to go where everybody knows your name," is somewhat appropriate for how many of us feel concerning church. We want to go to a place where we feel comfortable and welcomed, not to a place where people ignore us. Churches are sometimes surprised when they take a hard look at how welcoming they really are to strangers who visit. It is easy to talk only with those whom you are familiar while ignoring someone new who is unfamiliar.

An evangelistic community reflects the love of God to its visiting neighbors and to others they encounter. A community that is able to reflect this love consistently and continually will begin to see others react to them differently, more positively. Regardless of the size of your congregation one evangelism goal for each year should be improving on your hospitality to others. Wesley welcomed all and worked to make them feel welcomed. Are we doing the same today? Reflecting the love of God to our neighbors requires a congregation to be intentional in making sure your church is a place where at least somebody "knows your name."

REPORTING IT TO OTHERS

For Wesley, it is not only important to reflect the love of God to others, we also must report (tell) about this love to others. Some of us are willing to reflect God's love because that seems innocent and non-invasive. But we are God's heralds on earth. The Wesleyan way of evangelism calls for us to tell about this love to others. When Jesus healed the blind man in John 9:1-12 he kept telling to everyone about God's goodness. We, too, are called to report to others what God has done in our lives.

If we are called as Christians to report about God's love to others today, then how do we do this? In chapter five we talked about the power of testimony and letting people know where your story has intersected the gospel story. Critical to testifying and to reporting about God's goodness to others is establishing a relationship. The Wesleyan way of evangelism is relational and for others to hear your testimony it is necessary to have some form of a relationship with them. The relationship can be established over time or immediately as Jesus often did with those he encountered. People are willing to listen if they feel you care.

Jesus was not manipulative in establishing relationships with others and neither should we be. The man healed in John 9:1-12 had an audience because they could not believe he was the same person who used to beg every day. He did not go out and create an audience; people were willing to listen because of the transformation that took place in his life resulting from his encounter with Jesus. Others notice when there is something new about a person and will often ask the person what is different. Reporting to them the transformation God is doing in one's life is a legitimate way to express the love of God to others.

One of the challenges we encounter in reporting God's love to others is we are afraid of pushing our beliefs upon them. In American society today, what one believes is considered a private matter and others should not intrude into that area. It is easier for most of us not to broach the subject of beliefs than to tell others about God's love. Yet, if we follow Wesley's example, then we should constantly be telling others about God's love.

Reporting God's love to others is not an attempt on our part to fool, manipulate or force anyone into believing something different. It is instead an unapologetic and honest reporting of how we have experienced God's love and goodness. When God is transforming us it will shine through in ways we cannot imagine and bring us into relationships with individuals we could never imagine. Are we willing to love others by sharing with others God's love? The Wesleyan way of evangelism encourages us to tell of God's love and goodness so that all may experience God's transformation through Jesus the Christ.

RESPONDING TO GOD

As Christians we can reflect the love of God to others, we can report about God's love to others, but it is the Holy Spirit that helps someone to respond to God's love. Sometimes as Christians we become so determined to help someone enter into a relationship with Jesus the Christ that we forget the person is not responding to us, but to God. It is God who converts people, and does not force or manipulate anyone into entering into a relationship with Jesus. As we choose to be in relationship with other humans, we must choose to be in relationship with Jesus.

Wesley describes this freedom all humans have in entering into a relationship with Jesus:

> You know how God wrought in *your own* soul, when he first enabled you to say, "The life I now live, I live by faith in the Son of God, who loved me, and gave himself for me." He did not take away your understanding, but enlightened and strengthened it. He did not destroy any of your affections; rather they were more vigorous than before. Least of all did he take away your liberty, your power choosing good or evil; He did not *force* you; but, being *assisted* by his grace you, like Mary, *chose* the better part.[8]

Wesley uses some wonderful terms to make his point, but we especially like the sentence stating, "He did not take away your understanding, but enlightened and strengthened it." God's grace is not restricting, but enables us to discern clearer and to live freer lives. The beauty is God assists us in doing this through grace so we do not have to depend upon our own abilities. The mistake we make in life is thinking our reasoning is better than God's reasoning and we can depend on our own abilities.

One example that may help clarify Wesley's point is to think about recovery groups like Alcoholics Anonymous or drug rehab programs. Many of the meetings follow some form of a twelve step program where one of the initial steps is recognizing one's own inability to stop the abuse. In fact, although the program does not specifically name God's grace, it moves in that direction when claiming intervention from a higher power is necessary as part of the recovery process. The goal is for individuals to realize that trying to stop the abuse through their own actions is often futile and it is not until one is willing to open themselves to the higher power (God's grace) that recovery can begin.

Wesley did not develop a twelve step program for the recovery of the image of God, but the renewal of the image begins by our response to the Holy Spirit. For potential believers this means opening one's self to God's grace and responding to the Holy Spirit. It is recognizing one's own ability is limited and only by God's grace can we truly recover the image of God. For those in your congregation afraid of doing evangelism this is good news. Their job is not to force a response, but to invite a response by reflecting and reporting the love of God.

Spreading the good news means loving God and our neighbor cannot be just afterthoughts. We must practice as individuals and communities what it means to be in relationship with God and with our neighbors. It is only by being in relationship with God that we are transformed and can reflect and report that love to others. Wesley's success as an evangelist was in part because he worked every day to be in relationship with God and his neighbor. What would happen evangelistically in our churches if we rededicated ourselves to being in a deeper relationship with God and our neighbors?

Questions

1. What are the obstacles to evangelism in your church? How might you overcome these?

2. What hinders us from reporting God's love to others?

3. What challenges does your congregation face in relating to "neighbors?"

RELATIONAL
EVANGELISM

Throughout this book we have claimed evangelism the Wesleyan way is relational. The fundamental way that Wesley understood what it meant to be relational was through loving God and our neighbor. In exploring the Wesleyan way of evangelism and what it means for us today the acronym R.E.L.A.T.I.O.N.A.L., can be a helpful approach.

*R*enewal

Salvation for Wesley is our renewal in the image of God. Conversion is not the end of the journey, it is the beginning of one's transformation into the likeness of Christ. In other words, it is the beginning of one's renewal into the image of God. For Wesley, the goal is not claiming one is saved as an end in and of itself, but salvation signals a beginning whereby one starts the process of being renewed into a new being.

Renewal into the image of God does not take place overnight and it is not something we attain in the sense of an achievement. We continue to grow in grace daily by loving God and loving our neighbor. Unfortunately, many of us today in the church do not think about growing in grace daily, nor do we connect being renewed into the image of God with evangelism. Wesley does make this connection—he shifts the focus of evangelism from simply a single decisionistic model to one that involves a lifelong journey.

We testify to others not for them to "accept Christ" and think nothing else is necessary. We testify to others so that they can enter into a relationship with Christ and be renewed into the image of God. God's work of renewal continues throughout our Christian journey. In some ways, this should relieve the pressure of sharing one's faith because the goal is not to create a scorecard of how many people we convert. The goal is through loving our neighbor to share with them and to demonstrate to them that they too can experience the renewal of God's image in their lives.

Wesley sees God's work culminating in the renewal of the entire creation:

> All unprejudiced persons may see with their eyes, that He is already renewing the face of the earth: And we have strong reason to hope that the work he hath begun, he will carry on unto the day of the Lord Jesus; that he will never intermit this blessed work of his Spirit, until he has fulfilled all his promises, until he hath put a period to sin, and misery, and infirmity, and death, and re-established universal holiness and happiness, and caused all the inhabitants of the earth to sing together, "Hallelujah, the Lord God omnipotent reigneth!"[9]

God's work of renewal is continuing and will continue until Jesus returns. When we begin to be renewed into the image of God we experience a transformation that will one day encompass the entire earth.

*E*nter

The Wesleyan way of evangelism calls for us to help others enter into a relationship with Christ and a church community. Helping others to enter into a relationship with Christ is why we testify about the love of God. Yet entering into a relationship with Christ without also entering into a supporting and loving community can set a person up for failure. Someone who accepts Christ but never becomes a part of the community and thinks all they need is Jesus misses out on the new life that salvation is.

To enter into a relationship with Jesus is to become a part of the body of believers. We develop a personal relationship with Jesus, through which we become more Christlike. At the same time we develop relationships with others in the community who help us to strengthen and express our personal relationship with Jesus. Although not a perfect example, entering into marriage has similarities with starting a relationship with Jesus. A person marries another, committing to be faithful to that individual, but in marriage one usually has extended relationships with the family and friends of her/his spouse. Marriage is a commitment to one person that can create extended relationships by virtue of that commitment. Entering into a relationship with Jesus makes a personal commitment that creates extended relationships to others in the community.

As we discussed earlier in the book, two ways the Wesleys emphasized the importance of entering into a relationship with Jesus and the community is through Holy Communion and the Love Feast. For us today when we take Holy Communion we should remember God's action of coming not only to us, but also to others. We agree by partaking of the elements to participate with the others in the community toward making this world whole until Jesus returns. Evangelistically this is important because we are inviting people to not only experience the transformation that comes with being in a relationship with Jesus, but also to experience the transformation that comes with being in relationship with others who love God.

Listening

The Wesleyan way of evangelism requires us to listen to others in love. Sometimes people will seek out others because they are looking for someone to hear what is going on in their lives. Yet we can become so excited about wanting to tell others what God is doing in our lives that we do not take the time to listen to their story. An important aspect of evangelism is the ability to just listen without interjecting all we know about the gospel.

For instance, the tendency for many of us when we see someone begging on the street is to ignore them and walk by, to give them a little bit of money to get rid of them, and sometimes we even tell them where they can go for assistance. How many of us take the time to listen to their stories? Our lives are busy and usually we encounter people begging when we are in a hurry, but even when we have time we do not listen. Listening to others means we recognize their humanity and do not treat them as objects to be ignored or quickly dispensed.

But it is not just strangers we ignore—we often ignore those close to us. We do not want to hear their story because we are afraid it will require us getting involved. Evangelism within the Wesleyan tradition is relational so it requires a level of involvement with our neighbor. Effective evangelism does not require talking all the time and sometimes we may not need to talk at all. Learning to listen and hear the stories of others can be transforming not only for the hearer, but the one sharing.

Acceptance

One of the most powerful stories of acceptance (forgiveness) in the Bible is when Peter rejects Jesus three times before the crucifixion, and Jesus (in John 21:15ff.) asks Peter three times "do you love me—then feed my sheep." Peter is portrayed in most of the gospels as the outspoken disciple who is willing to do anything for Jesus. Yet in Jesus' greatest time of need it is Peter who denies any association with Jesus. This does not faze Jesus the Christ who welcomes Peter back with open arms.

God's acceptance of humanity is an act of grace. Evangelism within the Wesleyan tradition recognizes all of us need God's grace and this grace cannot be earned by us. Peter discovered all he did to please Jesus paled in comparison to Jesus' extension of grace to him after denying the Lord three times. Seekers sometimes feel that they must clean up their act so God will accept them. The good news we can share with others is they do not have to earn God's grace—it is given freely.

The power of God's acceptance should not be underestimated. Most of us long for acceptance from others in our lives, but only God can give truly unmerited acceptance. Evangelistically this means helping others to understand God's love for us is so pervasive that all are welcome no matter their situation. If Peter, who denied Jesus three times, experienced transformation because of God's unmerited acceptance, then we also can experience transformation and acceptance.

Testimony

The Wesleyan way of evangelism encourages us to tell others about God's love and the power of God's love to transform situations. Ultimately, the hope is everyone in a congregation will feel comfortable talking about what God is doing in their lives. The truth is this is not likely. An idea that may help concerning those who are not comfortable testifying verbally is writing their testimony down to be shared anonymously. People can write a one paragraph testimony about what God is doing in their lives and these can be put in the bulletin once a month for others to read, put on the church web page or church newsletter. The point is to give individuals an opportunity to testify in a way that may be more comfortable.

We emphasize testimony in this book, but is it really that important? Yes! We must be able to share with others what makes our relationship to Jesus central to our lives. We must be able to share with others how the church we attend helps us to grow in our relationship to Jesus and to live it out in a meaningful way. People are able to share why they root for a certain sports team over another team. People are able to share why they like a particular restaurant more than others. We should be able to share why the gospel intersecting with our lives is so important to us.

Getting people to testify to what God is doing in their lives needs to be an integral part of any evangelistic church plan. Others need to hear about God's transforming work and that God continues working. In a society where most of the news is negative, we need to hear some *good news*. Working with parishioners to testify about God's goodness is one way to spread some good news.

Inviting

The Wesleyan way of evangelism encourages communities to be inviting and open to others. Hospitality is one of the most important ministries in the church, but it is one that is often taken for granted. Very few churches believe they are closed and not inviting to others. Yet the actual actions by a congregation often tell a different story than the one they profess. Something all congregations can do to improve their evangelistic efforts is work on their hospitality.

An inviting community is also one that "invites" others to their church. It can be an invitation to a special event, a class or to a worship service. The important thing to do is to invite. Wesley invited those to whom he preached to a class meeting. If he preached and never extended an invitation, then few would have come or even known about the meetings. We need to invite others to come to church and not be afraid of the response we will receive.

A third place where invitation is needed is in transitional neighborhoods. Churches in transitional neighborhoods need to practice loving their neighbors by extending invitations to come participate in church events. An open church must truly be open to all God's people and not just those who used to live in the neighborhood. The possibilities for transformation when we invite others and treat them hospitably are more than we could fathom. Wesley said the world was his parish; some of us today do not need to look far in order to invite the world to our church.

On-going

One of the challenges with evangelism is people get excited for a while, but after some time goes by and the initial flame has dimmed, people tend to stop their evangelistic practices. Some may remember the children's story about the tortoise and the hare running a race and the hare who was much faster thinking the tortoise did not stand a chance. The hare went out quickly with great excitement, but burned out. The tortoise went out slower and kept a steady pace and eventually won the race. The swift do not always win the race.

Evangelism is not a race for how quickly one can do a program or complete a course. The Wesleyan way of evangelism is about a lifestyle change and a commitment to staying on the path of holiness. Evangelism is about the on-going commitment by all in the congregation to seek the renewal of the image of God in their lives and having the mind of Christ. Evangelism is about committing to loving God and neighbor. The evangelistic practices we are suggesting within the Wesleyan tradition are not things that can be checked off of a list so one can move on to something else. Wesley proposes a different way for us to live our lives so that others will be attracted to what we are doing and want to imitate us.

Wesley frequently uses the language of new birth to describe the transformation God works in our lives. He writes:

> It is the change wrought in the whole soul by the almighty Spirit of God when it is 'created anew in Christ Jesus', when it is 'renewed after the image of God', 'in righteousness and true holiness', when the love of the world is changed into the love of God, pride into humility, passion into meekness; hatred, envy, malice, into a sincere, tender, disinterested love for all mankind. In a word, it is that change whereby the 'earthly, sensual, devilish' mind is turned into 'the mind which was in Christ.'[2]

The transformation from the love of the world to the love of God does not occur overnight. We do not wake up one morning and decide we will "have the mind of Christ" from this point forward. Loving God and neighbor is a lifetime commitment and so are the evangelistic practices connected to practicing this love. The Wesleyan way of evangelism is not a race for the swift, but it is one for those committed to finishing the race no matter how long it takes.

New Beings

Makeovers are very popular currently. There are several television shows structured around the theme of makeovers. The general idea is someone (or something) looks one way and after the makeover the person looks completely new—a complete metamorphosis. The emphasis of most of these television shows is changing the outside appearance of a person. The truth is the person on the show probably did not go through a similar transformation of her/his character as she/he did of her/his outward appearance.

Christianity in general is concerned with humans becoming new people. Wesley encouraged people to change from having the character of this world to having a heart habitually filled with the love of God. The process of this change means becoming a new being no longer beholden to one's old ways. Evangelistically this is important because it means those who come in contact with us should experience us differently than they do others. Others should genuinely experience the love that emanates from us as a core part of who we are and not as something we put on as an outward appearance.

Wesley is clear that a heart truly transformed by God is concerned with more than outward appearances. One of the things we need to work on in the church today is helping people not to settle for outward appearances, but to allow the Holy Spirit to transform their hearts. For Christians, the Wesleyan way of evangelism means living as new beings and others seeing the change occurring in our lives. People today can tell if someone is just putting on an outward front or if they are sincere in what they are claiming. We must be sincere in our efforts to live as new beings and not just put on outward appearances. Although we experience God's transformation throughout our lives, we cannot wait until some future date to start living as the new person God is forming us into at the present.

*A*ssurance

One of the things we struggle with today in society is knowing what is real and what is just another fad. This is often true when it comes to our own lives in trying to figure out what we can be certain about. One of the challenges of evangelism is trying to express to others the certainty (assurance) we feel in a relationship with Jesus. In part, for evangelism, we need to help others to understand what we mean by assurance and why we can claim assurance in a relationship with Jesus.

Wesley often used the language of God's Spirit witnessing to our spirit in describing this notion of assurance. He writes:

> The testimony now under consideration is given by the Spirit of God to and with our spirit. He is the person testifying. What he testifies to us is 'that we are the children of God.' The immediate result of this testimony is 'the fruit of the Spirit'; namely, 'love, joy, peace; longsuffering, gentleness, goodness.' And without these the testimony itself cannot continue.[3]

Wesley argues we have assurance when we become children of God and we know this by the fruits of the Spirit. The assurance we have as believers is not one of exemption from the trials and tribulations of life. The assurance Wesley is talking about is a confidence that God has intersected with our story and because of this we know we are God's children.

Wesley uses the word testimony in the above quote—the same word we used throughout the book to describe sharing the faith with others. In both cases, the word points to an intersection of the divine with our human story. This is the assurance we have as believers that the Holy Spirit intersects with our story helping us to live as children of God. Others will recognize we are God's children because when we do face difficult life situations the fruits we produce will be in accordance with being formed into the image of God.

The Wesleyan way of evangelism encourages people to experience the intersection of the divine in their lives. It does not promise people by experiencing this intersection they will no longer face difficulties in life. We can testify to others we are God's children because God continues to testify to us through the Holy Spirit. The assurance that comes with being a child of God is grounded in our faith, hope, and especially love that we experience as we grow in our relationship to Jesus the Christ.

Live-it

The Wesleyan way of evangelism requires that we live evangelistic lives by loving our neighbors. Wesley's relational approach to evangelism centers on the way in which we live out what it means to be a disciple of Christ in practice. The reason we want to be renewed into the image of God, to testify to God's goodness, to help others understand the length God goes to forgive us (acceptance), etc., is for us to be able to live transformed lives. Living an evangelistic life means daily we seek to love God and our neighbor with everything in us. There are no vacation days or time off from living a life that is truly given to loving God and neighbor.

For Wesley, the works of piety and the works of mercy help people to stay focused on loving God and neighbor. Reclaiming this Wesleyan way of thinking about loving God and neighbor can be helpful for congregations today. The works of piety help us to love God with our whole heart, mind, body and soul. The works of mercy help us to love our neighbor as ourselves. Yet, these are not two separate ways of loving, but one way of loving that helps us to move toward holiness—becoming whole individuals. We evangelize to help people to become whole individuals and truly human in the manner that God intended.

This is not becoming whole by human standards. This is a wholeness based upon what it means to love God and neighbor by living transformed lives. It is seeking to have the mind of Christ in our daily journey. In his sermon, "The Almost Christian," Wesley says those who are "almost a Christian" do what the gospel prescribes and have the outward appearance of a Christian.[4] He contrasts these individuals with "altogether Christians" and the big difference is in how they love God and neighbor.

The way in which we live out the love of God and neighbor is what distinguishes us as Christians. It therefore must distinguish our evangelistic efforts. As Christians we cannot pick who to love and who is acceptable to God; we must love all people and reflect God's love to them.

Wesley writes about loving our neighbors:

If any man ask, "Who is my neighbor?" we reply, 'Every man in the world; every child of his who is "the Father of the spirits of flesh."' Nor may we in any wise except our enemies or the enemies of God and their own souls. But every Christian loveth these also as himself; yea, "as Christ loved us."[5]

Congregations that are able to help individuals to love in this manner will become evangelistic and notice a difference in their parishioners. Congregations who are living evangelistic lives may not see a huge growth in church numbers, but the parishioners will be making a difference in the lives of people wherever they come in contact with them. If congregations do nothing else suggested in this book, the one thing they should do is to encourage people to live evangelistic lives—lives that demonstrate to others the true transforming power of loving God and neighbor.

Final Thoughts

The Wesley way of evangelism is relational. It is about loving God and neighbor and the transformation that is possible when we are truly loving. It is about encouraging people to become whole and to be renewed into the image of God. It is about understanding the power of our testimonies and how they can encourage others. It is about understanding God will accept us no matter what our situation.

Perhaps Charles said it best in his hymn "Love Divine, All Loves Excelling." The words to his hymn should inspire us to love God and neighbor—the Wesleyan way of evangelism:

Love Divine, all loves excelling, joy of heaven to earth come down; Fix in us thy humble dwelling; all thy faithful mercies crown! Jesus thou art all compassion, pure, unbounded love thou art; visit us with thy salvation; enter every trembling heart.

Breathe, o breathe thy loving Spirit into every troubled breast! Let us all in thee inherit; let us find that second rest. Take away our bent to sinning; Alpha and Omega be; end of faith, as its beginning, set our hearts at liberty.

Come, Almighty to deliver, let us all thy life receive; suddenly return and never, never more thy temples leave. Thee we would be always blessing, serve thee as thy hosts above, pray and praise thee without ceasing, glory in thy perfect love.

Finish, then, thy new creation; pure and spotless let us be. Let us see thy great salvation perfectly restored in thee; changed from glory into glory, till in heaven we take our place, till we cast our crowns before thee, lost in wonder, love, and praise.[6]

Questions:

1. How are you experiencing God's renewal in your life? How can you share your experiences with others?

2. How can we become better listeners?

3. What event can you invite others to come experience at your church?

4. How can you more intentionally live an evangelistic life?

5. What images of love does the Charles Wesley hymn conjure up for you?

STUDY GUIDE

Six Week Study

Week 1:
Focus: An overview of the Wesleyan way of evangelism and evangelism in general.
Read: Introduction, Chapter One and Chapter Two

Week 2:
Focus: Developing a Wesleyan evangelistic community.
Read: Chapter Three

Week 3:
Focus: Integrating Wesley's understanding of works of piety and mercy into our evangelistic practices.
Read: Chapter Four

Week 4:
Focus: Sharing and embodying the word of God.
Read: Chapter Five

Week 5:
Focus: Relational evangelism within the Wesleyan tradition.

Read: Chapter Six

Week 6:
What will we do differently as believers after studying this book? What ideas can we integrate into the life of our congregation?

NOTES

CHAPTER 1

1. John Wesley, "An Earnest Appeal to Men of Reason and Religion" par. 2. *Works* 11:45.

2. Ibid.

3. Ibid, par. 3, 11:45.

4. Ibid, par. 4, 11:46.

5. Ronald J. Sider, *The Scandal of the Evangelical Conscience: Why Are Christians Living Just Like the Rest of the World?* (Grand Rapids: Baker Book House, 2005), 58.

6. John Wesley, "The Scripture Way of Salvation," par. I.l, *Works* 2:156.

7. O Love Divine, What Hast Thou Done, *The United Methodist Hymnal* (Nashville: The United Methodist Publishing House, 1989) 287.

CHAPTER 2

1. John Wesley, "An Earnest Appeal to Men of Reason and Religion," par. 9, *Works* 11:48

2. H. Eddie Fox & George E. Morris, *Faith-Sharing,* [revised & expanded edition] (Nashville: Discipleship Resources, 1996), 53-54.

3. John Wesley, "The Nature, Design, and General Rules of the United Societies," par. 4-6, *Works* 9:70-73.

4. John Wesley, "On Dissipation," par. 6, *Works* 3:118.

5. John Wesley, "On Dissipation," par. 12, *Works* 3:120

6 . John Wesley, "On Living Without God," par. 7, *Works* 4:171.

7. George G. Hunter III, *How to Reach Secular People* (Nashville: Abingdon Press, 1992), 76-77.

8. Ibid, 81-83.

9. See Steven W. Manskar, *Accountable Discipleship: Living in God's Household* (Nashville: Discipleship Resources, 2000) and Gayle Turner

Watson, *Guide for Covenant Discipleship Groups* (Nashville: Discipleship Resources, 2000).

10. William J. Abraham, *The Logic of Evangelism* (Grand Rapids: William B. Eerdmans, 1989). 95.

11. Scott J. Jones, *The Evangelistic Love of God & Neighbor: A Theology of Witness and Discipleship* (Nashville: Abingdon Press, 2003), 114.

12. John Wesley, "The New Birth," par. IV.4, *Works* 2:199.

13. Daniel T. Benedict Jr., *Come to the Waters: Baptism & Our Ministry of Welcoming Seekers & Making Disciples* (Nashville: Discipleship Resources, 1996).

14. Robert E. Webber, *Journey to Jesus: The Worship, Evangelism, and Nurture Mission of the Church* (Nashville: Abingdon Press, 2001). See also his *Ancient-Future Evangelism: Making Your Church a Faith-Forming Community* (Grand Rapids: Baker Book House, 2003).

CHAPTER 3

1. John Wesley, preface to "Hymns and Sacred Poems," *Works,* 14:321.

2. H. Eddie Fox & George E. Morris, *Faith-Sharing* [Revised & expanded edition] (Nashville: Discipleship Resources, 1996), 55.

3. John Wesley, "A Plain Account of The People Called Methodists," I.11, *Works* 9:259.

4. John Wesley, "A Plain Account," II.3, *Works* 9:260.

5. Ibid.

6. Randy Maddox, *Responsible Grace: John Wesley's Practical Theology* (Nashville: Abingdon Press, 1994), 210.

7. John Wesley, "A Plain Account," III.1, *Works* 9:264.

8. Albert C. Outler, *Evangelism In The Wesleyan Spirit* (Nashville: Discipleship Resources, 1996, 2000), 22.

9. Theodore Runyon, *The New Creation: John Wesley's Theology Today* (Nashville: Abingdon Press, 1998), 224.

10. Ibid.

11. Manfred Marquardt, *John Wesley's Social Ethics: Praxis and Principles* (Nashville: Abingdon, 1992), 30.

12. John Wesley, "On Visiting the Sick," I.1, *Works*, 3:387.

13. John Wesley, "A Plain Account," II.1, *Works,* 9:260.

14. Ibid.

15. John Wesley, "A Farther Appeal to Men of Reason and Religion," I.3, *Works*, 11:106.

16. Randy Maddox, *Responsible Grace*, 145.

17. John Wesley, "A Collection of Hymns," *Works*, 7:698.

18. Ibid.

19. Jesus, Lord, We Look to Thee, *The United Methodist Hymnal* (Nashville: The United Methodist Publishing House, 1989), 562.

CHAPTER 4

1. For more on the means of grace see Henry H. Knight III, *Eight Life-Enriching Practices of United Methodists* (Nashville: Abingdon Press, 2001); Steve Harper, *Prayer and Devotional Life of United Methodists* (Nashville: Abingdon Press, 1999), and Steve Harper, *Devotional Life in the Wesleyan Tradition* (Nashville: The Upper Room, 1983).

2. John Wesley, *Journal*, May 24, 1738, par. 14, *Works* 18:249-250.

3. John Wesley, "The Witness of the Spirit I," par. I.7, *Works*, l:274.

4. John Wesley, "The Witness of the Spirit II,", par. II.6, *Works* l:287-288

5. Ibid., par. V.3, *Works* 1:297-98.

6. Ibid., par. V.4, *Works* 1:298

7. Spirit of Faith, Come Down, *The United Methodist Hymnal* (Nashville: The United Methodist Publishing House, 1989), 332.

CHAPTER 5

1. John Wesley, "Journal," *Works* 18:249-250.

2. Another place to reference the idea of the Word becoming Flesh is in chapter 12, H. Eddie Fox and George E. Morris, *Let the Redeemed of the Lord Say So! Invitational Witnessing for the New Millennium* (Franklin, Tennessee: Providence House Publishers, 1999, 1991).

3. John Wesley, "Journal," *Works* 19:46.

4. John Wesley, "Journal," *Works* 21:230.

5. Ibid.

6. John Wesley, "Journal," *Works* 21:473.

7. 'Tis Finished! The Messiah Dies, *The United Methodist Hymnal* (Nashville: The United Methodist Publishing House, 1989), 282.

8. Kenneth H. Carter, Jr., *A Way of Life in the World: Spiritual Practices for United Methodists* (Nashville: Abingdon Press, 2004), 67.

9. John Wesley, "On Visiting the Sick," III.7, *Works* 3:396.

10. Runyon, *The New Creation*, 194.

11. John Wesley, "Journal," *Works* 22:169-170.

12. Henry H. Knight III, *Eight Life-Enriching Practices of United Methodists* (Nashville: Abingdon Press, 2001), 61.

13. Frank Baker, *Methodism And The Love-Feast* (London: Epworth Press, 1957), 25.

14. John Wesley, "Journal," *Works* 21:335-336.

15. Freedom Train a-Comin', *Songs of Zion* (Nashville: Abingdon Press, 1981) 92.

16. John Wesley, "Journal," *Works* 24:13.

17. John Wesley, "Journal," *Works* 23:31.

18. O For a Thousand Tongues to Sing, *The United Methodist Hymnal* (Nashville: The United Methodist Publishing House, 1989), 57.

CHAPTER 6

1. Jones, *Evangelistic Love of God & Neighbor,* 51.

2. John Wesley, "The Character of A Methodist," paragraph 5, *Works* 9:35.

3. Runyon, *The New Creation*, 13.

4. Ibid.

5. John Wesley, "The Circumcision of the Heart," II.10, *Works* 1:413-14.

6. John Wesley, "On Love," II.2, *Works* 4:383.

7. Roger K. Swanson and Shirley F. Clement, *The Faith-Sharing Congregation: Developing a Strategy for the Congregation as Evangelist* (Nashville: Discipleship Resources, 1999), 17.

8. John Wesley, "The General Spread of the Gospel," 11, *Works* 2:489.

Chapter 7

1. John Wesley, "The General Spread of the Gospel," 27, Works 2:499.

2. John Wesley, The New Birth, " II.5, *Works* 2:194.

3. John Wesley, "The Witness of the Spirit II," II.1, *Works* 1:286.

4. John Wesley, "The Almost Christian," II.4, *Works* 1:138-39.

5. John Wesley, "The Almost Christian," II.2, *Works* 1:137-138.

6. Love Divine, All Loves Excelling, *The United Methodist Hymnal* (Nashville: The United Methodist Publishing House, 1989), 384.